HAUNTED TENNESSEE

Charles Edwin Price

Illustrations and Photography
by the Author

The Overmountain Press

JOHNSON CITY, TENNESSEE

ISBN 1-57072-037-1
Copyright ©1995 by Charles Edwin Price
All Rights Reserved
Printed in The United States of America

4 5 6 7 8 9 0

For
MELANIE & MELISSA

Other books by Charles Edwin Price

Folklore

Haints, Witches and Boogers:
Tales from Upper East Tennessee

The Day They Hung The Elephant

Demon In The Woods:
Tall Tales and True from East Tennessee

The Mystery of Ghostly Vera
And Other Haunting Tales of Southwest Virginia

Haunted Jonesborough

I'd Rather Have A Talking Frog:
Tales From Johnson City

The Infamous Bell Witch of Tennessee

Fiction

Danger Train

Something Evil Lurks In The Woods

TABLE OF CONTENTS

Acknowledgments vii

Introduction ix

Woodland Sprites, Water Spirits, and Monsters. 1

Out of Their Graves There Grew a Tree. 9

The Ghosts of Tennessee High 13

The Ghostly Gun Battle 17

Unquiet Graves?. 23

The Phantom Horse 29

The Library Ghost 34

A Haunted Organ 37

Footprints in the Snow 43

The Haunted Rock 48

Haunted Sam Houston 53

Something Is Trying to Get Through the Floor! 59

The Bell Witch of Tennessee 62

The Ghost of Port Royal 79

Ghost Lights of the Cumberlands 84

Something Horrible Is Peering in the Window 91

Devil May Care 96

The Ghost Who Wanted a Hug 102

A Fate Worse Than Death 110

Long Live the King 122

Darkman 127

ACKNOWLEDGMENTS

I'd like to thank everyone who helped me put this volume of Tennessee ghost stories together. Of course some of the contributors asked that their names not be mentioned, and I've respected their wishes.

I would also like to thank my long-suffering editor at The Overmountain Press, Sherry Lewis, for her astounding patience and unassailable skill in whipping this book into shape.

Finally I'd like to thank my wife, Patty, for her encouragement, my daughters, Melanie and Melissa, for consistently invading my den when I was in the throes of creativity, and my favorite cat, Clinton, for placing his mark (mainly paw prints) on the manuscript and haphazardly careening around the den in pursuit of the our other cat, Toledo (aka "Prune Face"); and also to my dog, Gilligan, who will probably never understand that two doggie treats at a time are more than enough because tomorrow is another day.

INTRODUCTION

Ghost stories fascinate me to death. I love to sit by a fireplace on a cold winter's night, or around a blazing campfire in the woods in summer, and listen to someone spin ghastly tales of apparitions, witches, goblins, long-legged beasties, and things that go bump in the night.

I come by this taste honestly. My grandfather must have known a hundred creepy tales, and he told them often when I was a little boy. Most of his stories were set in rural Maryland where I grew up—back in the "dark ages," when movie admission was twenty cents and the price of a Coke was still a nickel.

One tale in particular had an extraordinary effect on my ability to sleep at night. That was the frightful saga of a nocturnal creature called the "snallyghaster"—part bird, part reptile, all meanness.

Papaw said the snallyghaster wolfed down full-grown men in a single gulp. I was told the snallyghaster was especially fond of Boy Scouts, but Papaw never told me the reason for this particular druther. However, the fact weighed heavily on my imagination, especially during the years I participated in scout camporees on South Mountain.

At night, around blazing campfires, scouts told each other ghost stories. When my turn to tell a story came around, I never failed to recount Papaw's tale of the snallyghaster, and it never failed so send chills up the young spines of normally "fearless" Boy Scouts.

Afterwards, lying in the darkness of my pup tent, I was always on guard for the irrefutable sign of the ravenous snallyghaster—when all the night birds stopped singing at once. When that occurred, a snallyghaster was sure to be lurking nearby.

When Papaw died at age ninety-one, his tales died with him. Unfortunately no one ever wrote them down. Today I can remember only bits and pieces, but not one complete story. The great tragedy of my life was that neither I, nor anyone else in my family, ever understood the value of Papaw's ghost tales—that is until it was too late to do anything about preserving them!

In Tennessee, folks have told ghost stories for hundreds of years. And even before settlers crossed the rugged Allegheny Mountains and built the first cabin in the fertile Nolichucky and Holston valleys, American Indians told spine-tingling tales of terror around their own campfires.

Thousands of these Indian ghost stories have been forgotten over the years. The Cherokee Indians had no written language until Sequoyah invented the syllabary in the early nineteenth century. Indians passed on stories orally.

Whites, too, had their own oral storytelling tradition. Since nearly all original settlers were immigrants to the New World, homesteaders brought stories from their native lands. At first Indians were friendly to the white invaders and would join them at their hearths—and vice versa. And since the New World was a melting pot for an array of European cultures, there was naturally a meshing of various stories. All these tales—Indian, English, Irish, Scot, French, German—merged into what we now call American folklore.

It would be difficult to imagine the sheer volume of tales that probably once existed. Many are forgotten—lost in the mists of time. But thousands more are remembered and continue to be told orally by fathers to their sons, by mothers to their daughters. As a body of oral literature, folk stories tell much about who we are as Tennesseans and where we came from. Tennessee's rich heritage is reflected in these stories.

The stories in this book are part of a subcategory of folklore called "ghostlore." What does ghostlore include?

Ghostlore includes "real-life" tales about ghosts, goblins, witches, and demons that people once believed in and, perhaps, still do. A person may live in a house where strange, unexplained noises are heard—moaning, footsteps, doors opening and closing by themselves. Or inanimate objects may move without benefit of human assistance. Some may have actually seen a ghost—a wispy phantom floating down a stairwell or through a darkened hallway. The apparition may have even spoken. When one person tells another of a frightening experience, he is passing on ghostlore. (See "Unquiet Graves.")

Ghostlore includes made-up stories that are told for sake of effect. When pioneer parents wanted to insure that their children stayed close to the cabin, they told them tales of demons, ghosts, and witches lurking in the surrounding forest. These tales scared the children and kept them from wandering off in the woods by themselves. (The real terrors of the forest—bears, wildcats, poisonous reptiles, marauding Indians, etc.—apparently didn't faze children at all.) Cherokee Indians often told their own children stories about evil spirits that bedeviled the living. The Devil's Looking Glass, a three hundred-foot cliff overlooking the Nolichucky River, located about ten miles east of Jonesborough in Unicoi County, is said to have evil spirits lurking in a cave about halfway up the face. The Cherokee used stories to warn others away from the treacherous cliff. (See "Woodland Sprites, Water Spirits, and Monsters.")

"Lovers' Lane" tales, another kind of ghostlore, are especially plentiful. These are made-up stories that young men have told their girlfriends for hundreds of years—from the days of horses and wagons to modern-day automobiles. The tales are designed to frighten the girl so she will sit closer to the boy for protection. The premise probably sounds silly on the surface, but these stories are amazingly effective. (See "A Fate Worse Than Death.")

Ghostlore has sometimes been used as an excuse to "solve" mysteries that are impossible to solve logically. In the early days of this state, for example, a well unexpectedly drying up or the sudden sickness of livestock might be blamed on a witch's curse. There are people living in Tennessee who still believe in witches' curses. (See "Devil May Care.")

Whatever the origin of—or the reason for—the story, ghostlore is as intrinsic to Tennessee as corn bread and grits.

I personally like the "real-life" ghost stories best. These are supposed to be true events told by someone who actually experienced them. Many more have secondhand knowledge of someone else's experience.

A number of people have made lifetime studies of so-called "real-life" ghosts. In studying the tales, they have discovered—believe it or not—that there is a certain logic in nearly every "real-life" haunting. It's called "ghost logic."

Although there are certainly exceptions to the rule, most ghosts follow established patterns of behavior. Here are some typical examples of ghost logic:

The person most likely to become a ghost...

1. Was murdered
2. Committed suicide
3. Was unlucky in love
4. Vowed vengeance on someone before death
5. Was very evil in life
6. Died before an important task was finished
7. Had a very strong personality in life
8. Is searching for a lost loved one

Ghosts usually repeat the same behavior over and over again, like an endless loop of video tape. Behavior seldom varies from one sighting to the other. It's as if the ghost is acting out a single moment in its previous life.

Ghosts sometimes talk to the living but are seldom capable of carrying on an intelligent conversation. They say the same thing over and over again.

Seldom are ghosts seen in broad daylight. They almost always prefer the shadows.

Ghosts are heard more than seen. Mysterious noises (footsteps, pounding, etc.) are much more common than actual sightings of apparitions.

Believe it or not, ghosts can sometimes be reasoned with. In Jonesborough, Tennessee, a number of historic houses are presently being renovated. This activity seems to cause ghosts to rebel at the noise and dust. But homeowners are often able to talk to the ghost and tell it that the renovation is good for the house. Afterward, the ghostly activity usually stops.

There are more ghosts of women than of men. Children's ghosts are rare, but they exist. Ghosts of famous (and infamous) people are more plentiful than ghosts of everyday people—especially if the ghost was a firebrand in life (like, for example, Andrew Jackson).

Many ghosts are mischievous. (This is especially true of the ghosts of children.) They hide items like jewelry or important papers—often when their owners need them the most. Sometimes they even steal food. The stolen items, however, are almost always returned.

If a person sees a ghost and tries to talk to it, most of the time the ghost will instantly disappear.

Most of the tales contained in this book are new to print. I have tried to include stories that originate from what folklorists call "primary sources." These were tales told to me by individuals who have had firsthand experience with the ghosts or mysterious events they describe. They are the folks who live in haunted houses or can relate allegedly true tales of personal encounters with witches, demons, or other denizens of the supernatural.

In some cases the names have been changed at the request of the informer because of fear of ridicule. Unfortunately certain people are not very open-minded when it comes to the possible existence of ghosts.

In *Haunted Tennessee* you will also find tales that are plainly figments of someone's imagination—bloody tales from lovers' lanes, stories pioneer parents told their children to frighten them into staying close to the cabin, and stories designed to be told around a campfire for entertainment.

Additionally I have included interesting sidelights on the nature of ghosts, witches, vampires, and the like, backgrounds on the stories, trivia, and plenty of photographs and drawings.

I have, however, tried to avoid detailed yarns from Tennessee's largest towns and famous hauntings—with the possible exception of an account of the Bell Witch. (Several of my readers threatened to throttle me if I did not included this story!) My goal in this book was to tell of little-known hauntings, and retell tales that have not heretofore been published.

As Tennessee enters its bicentennial year, these stories become even more important. In 1996 Tennesseans will be reflecting on their heritage, and ghost tales are very much a part of that. The stories, superstitions, and traditions you will read in this book constitute only a small portion of a much larger picture—one that I hope will be fully explored during Tennessee's 200th birthday.

Charles Edwin Price
Erwin, Tennessee
Fall 1995

WOODLAND SPRITES, WATER SPIRITS, AND MONSTERS

We'll begin at the beginning—well, almost. The Cherokee Indians were not the first to occupy East Tennessee; but they were, by far, the best organized and most powerful of the early settlers. In fact some archaeologists and historians contend that by the time the first white men settled their land, the Cherokee's level of civilization was nearly equal to the Mayan, Aztec, and Inca nations of Central and South America.

The folklore of American Indians was highly refined, imaginative, and organized. Their folklore centered around the things that affected them most—the creation of the world, humanity, hunting, and food gathering. Therefore, it was not surprising that legends sprang up around such commonplace items as cultivated plants, or that elaborate ceremonies and rituals would be practiced by the Indians to celebrate the spirits that controlled their growth.

Animals, too, were revered and worshiped. When a Cherokee hunter killed a deer for food he would ask its pardon, explaining that his family was hungry and that the killing was necessary. The Indians considered animals conscious beings with whom it was necessary to establish rapport.

Cherokee folklore contained more than its share of mystical creatures like woodland sprites, waterspirits, and monsters.

The Cherokee Indians were a spiritual people who believed

that all things in nature had a soul, even inanimate objects like pools of water or great valleys. The rocks, mountains, and trees all had spirits. Every animal was a conscious being and had its own spirit. Even the land itself had a spirit. It had been created exclusively for the Cherokee but could not be possessed by any individual.

If any group ever belonged to or totally respected the environment, it was the Cherokee Indian.

But along with the good spirits there were evil ones, and the Indian had to be constantly on his guard not to be consumed by something horrible.

The Cherokee mostly lived in permanent towns along the Little Tennessee and Hiawasse rivers. The entire Cherokee Nation consisted of about 20,000 people who ranged over 40,000 square miles. Their territory included portions of Kentucky, Virginia, North Carolina, South Carolina, Georgia, Alabama, and Tennessee. Most of this was considered hunting ground. The Cherokee needed a wide area to spread out.

The population of each of the towns, located mostly along the banks of the Little Tennessee River, ranged from 200 to 500 people. Central to each town was a log council house, a seven-sided affair that housed a ceremonial fire that burned twenty-four hours a day. Each of the sides represented one of the seven clans—Wild Potato, Paint, Blue, Deer, Bird, Wolf, and Long Hair.

Inside the council house, members of each of the clans sat together, and several hundred people could be gathered together under one roof at the same time. Meetings of tribal importance were held in the council house. Town business was conducted. War councils were held.

Although a spiritual people, the nearest thing the Cherokee had to the clergy was the Adawehi or medicine man. To prevent evil spirits (boogers) from entering the council house and causing mischief, Adawehis wore horrifying masks (called "booger masks") that were supposed to frighten bugbears away.

Furthermore, spirits and demons lurked in the woods surrounding the towns, waiting for an opportunity to pounce on the unsuspecting. Some would even steal into town and kidnap children.

The Cherokee were so preoccupied with the presence of evil—or the eradication of it—that they had a hundred ways to purify their souls and bodies. One of these ways was called "going to water."

Indians believed that a river was a necessary element in the creation of a paradise on Earth. Immediately after birth a baby would be dipped in the river—no matter what the water's temperature. Daily immersions were routine until the child was about two years old.

But regular dunkings didn't stop there. Even as adults the Cherokee continued daily washings, not only to cleanse away sweat and dirt but to wash away evil as well.

Rivers were intrinsic to Cherokee religion. When young Cherokee males were about to become men, they would spend the night in a log shed, heated to an almost unbearable temperature. There the Adawehis would teach him the myths and traditions of the nation. At dawn the young Cherokees would be taken from the hot shed to the nearby river. Then, while the Adawehis recited prayers and incantations on the bank, the young Indians would wade into the water, face the rising sun, and immerse themselves seven times.

Even in the dead of winter, immersion in the river did the Indian little harm. James Adair, a British trader who lived with the Indians for twenty-eight years, wrote that the immersion made the Indian "almost as impenetrable as a bar of steel." This was proven over and over again. For example, one war party of Cherokee Indians swam the Ohio River in the middle of a snowstorm to attack their enemies on the other side.

Another method of purification was taking the sacred asi, or sacred "Black Drink," each morning after immersion. This potent concoction, brewed by boiling the roasted leaves, tops, and shoots of the winterberry—*Ilex vomitoria*—was an ominous dark liquid with white foam flecked on top. The drinker's first reaction to the asi was to throw up. The Indians believed the vomiting not only cleansed the body of evil, but strengthened it.

Although the rivers of Cherokee country were intrinsic to the purification of the soul, they also held danger. Of course the Indians realized that carelessness in the water could result in drowning. But they also believed that horrible monsters lurked in the depths. One of these was a gargantuan fish called the Dakwa.

The Dakwa lived in a deep pool of water, a few hundred yards downstream from the point where the Tellico River empties into the Little Tennessee. While sweating it out in the hot shed, young Indians were told this story by the Adawehis, which sounds suspiciously like the Biblical tale of Jonah and the "whale."

* * *

One day a canoe filled with warriors was floating down the river when the Dakwa suddenly raised up out of the water and tipped the canoe. The warriors swam for shore with all their might, and all made it to the bank but one. He was swallowed whole by the Dakwa.

When the warrior finally came to his senses inside the belly of the fish, he realized he was uninjured. He must try to escape.

It was hot and stifling inside the Dakwa and was so dark that he could not see. He reached for his knife but it wasn't there. He had lost it in the struggle.

The warrior felt around the belly of the fish for something to cut with. Finally his hands touched something sharp— whole mussel shells that the fish had swallowed. Finding the one with the sharpest edge, he proceeded to hack away at the stomach of the Dakwa.

Suddenly racked with sharp pains, the Dakwa began thrashing around. Water flew in all directions and covered the warriors watching the spectacle from the bank. The fish swam from one side of the pool to the other, roaring in agony.

Inside, the warrior continued cutting. Hot juices from the monster's belly engulfed him and burned his skin, but he continued cutting his way out of the belly of the fish.

Just as he thought he would perish inside the fish, the warrior felt a rush of cold water, then saw light through the hole. He was almost out.

The warrior resumed his cutting with renewed vigor. The hole got bigger and bigger. The violent movements of the pain-racked fish threw the warrior off balance, but he regained his feet and continued cutting.

Then he felt something hot and sticky—the monster's blood. The Dakwa was not moving as much. The warrior now had a hole hacked in the side of the fish just big enough to squeeze through. Above him he saw only blue sky, and he knew the monster was lying on its side, probably dying.

The warrior wiggled through the hole in the side of the fish. Once outside its body, he rolled into the cool water of the river and swam to the shore to rejoin his friends.

When he stood up and looked toward the fish, he saw it twitching in its final death spasm. He looked back to his friends, who were murmuring among themselves and pointing to him.

"What is wrong?" he asked one of them.

"Look into the river at your reflection," he was told.

He turned and looked into a still place at the river's edge. His eyes widened in amazement. The Dakwa's digestive juices had turned his dark skin and black hair pure white.

Although the warrior lived to be a very old man, he would always have white hair and skin!

* * *

The Cherokee believed in evil spirits. These, too, lurked in the water or in the forest. But the majority of these creatures lived in the folds of cliffs and in mountain hollows. Evil spirits especially liked hollows in the rock behind waterfalls. They hated the sunlight, and the majority of them were active only after dark.

One place where nefarious spirits lurked—and perhaps still do—was a 300-foot-tall rock cliff located on the Nolichucky River near the Unicoi/Washington County line. Called "The Devil's Looking Glass," the cliff was so infamous for the spirits living there that the Indians avoided it whenever possible. Even war parties floating down the Nolichucky River in canoes would refuse to look at its sheer rock face while they paddled past as quickly as possible.

It was said that a warrior who had dishonored his tribe climbed to the top of the Looking Glass one day and flung himself off the summit. His troubled spirit was rumored to inhabit the cliff and would lure other warriors to jump—sort of a misery loves company attitude.

Local tradition also claims that a cave, located about halfway up the face, is the home of the terrible "Demon with the Iron Finger." This unsavory character could take the shape of any living being and lure his prey into the cave. There the demon would lull his victim into a sound sleep. Then he would puncture the body with his iron finger and eat the lungs and liver of the unfortunate person.

There are literally thousands of Indian tales of demons, boogers, evil spirits, and the like in existence in Tennessee. Before the white man even landed on the shores of the New World, the Indians had a rich ghostlore of their own. Sometimes the settlers adapted these Indian tales, absorbing parts of them into their own tales from the Old World. These stories were stirred into the great cultural cauldron of diverse traditions and became what is now known as Appalachian folklore.

The Devil's Looking Glass, located on the Nolichucky River near the
Unicoi/Washington County border, is said to have evil spirits living in
the cracks of the rocks.

The Cherokee were a religious people. Nature was their cathedral and every living thing contained a "spirit" to be eulogized. Sunrise was the favored time for mystic ceremonies centered around the trees of the forest. Like the Druids of England, the Cherokee felt that trees contained a consciousness of their own. And they were said to absorb the psyche of people who died beneath their branches. Tales of trees haunted by human souls are rife in Indian lore.

OUT OF THEIR GRAVES
THERE GREW A TREE

Often plants have a certain mysticism about them. The mandrake, a wild plant that grows in Europe and Asia, is said to shed blood and scream whenever its root is plucked from the ground. Members of the nightshade family (which include the potato, tomato, petunia and belladonna) were once associated with witchcraft.

Due to tradition, certain plants symbolize human feelings and conditions, and sometimes they take on mystic qualities. A famous old English song called "Barbara Ellen" is a case in point.

"Barbara Ellen" recounts the tragic tale of a boy who loved a certain girl with all his heart. But the girl considered him beneath her dignity and ignored him. The boy did everything he could to prove to Barbara that he loved her and that he was worthy, but nothing worked. Finally, in despair, the boy killed himself for "the love of Barbara Ellen."

Barbara was so filled with remorse that a young man should commit suicide for her love, she promptly did herself in.

Both young people were buried in an old churchyard. Over the grave of the boy there grew a rose which symbolized the purity and self-sacrifice of his love. Over the grave of hard-hearted Barbara Ellen, of course, there grew a briar.

Spontaneous vegetation growing over the graves of doomed lovers—whether they be roses or briars or eucalyptus trees—

are generally symbolic of the true motives of the people when alive. In folklore, the bodies are almost always interred in forgotten or ill-kept graves, covered with weeds and undergrowth. Likewise, tragic figures are often buried in forgotten burial plots.

But there are exceptions to this. Sometimes a symbolic tree or bush is intentionally planted over such graves. Near Athens, on the campus of Tennessee Wesleyan College in McMinn County, lie the stumps of two ancient trees planted by an old Indian chief as a memorial for the two people that he loved the most.

It all started at a place called Fort Loudoun in the days when the French claimed the majority of the land that was to become Tennessee.

In 1754 war broke out between the French and English in a battle over the ownership of the Ohio Valley. Each side attempted to win aid from the various Indian tribes.

The Cherokee Nation, because of an agreement made with George II in 1730, first sided with the English. Actually it didn't mean a thing to them who they fought for or against. War, to the Cherokee, was a kind of vocation—an intrinsic part of their lifestyle that they enjoyed. They loved fighting and would go off on the warpath at the drop of a feather.

In the meantime, other tribes sided with the French. Some of these tribes were the very ones the Cherokee had fought throughout the years, and they harbored bitter feelings of revenge. Cherokee villages were raided by rival tribes loyal to the French while Cherokee warriors were out fighting for the English.

The raids caused the Overhill Cherokees to demand that the English build a fort to protect their women and children while the braves were out fighting. In 1757 the English from the South Carolina colony built Fort Loudoun, located at the mouth of the Tellico River, on the south bank of the Little Tennessee.

In the meantime the war was going badly for the French,

and in desperation they began telling the Cherokee that the English, if they were the victors, planned to settle Indian land, build forts and cabins, and drive out all the game. The French, on the other hand, reassured the Indians that they only wanted to trade and were not interested in settlement.

In 1759 the panicky Cherokee raided English settlements, killing and scalping settlers. Then the Indians laid siege to Fort Loudoun and starved the English garrisoned there into surrender. When the English soldiers attempted to leave the fort, they were ambushed by the Indians.

One wounded officer staggered into an Indian village. The chief took pity on him, and the old man's daughter, Nocatula, nursed him back to health. Why the officer—given the belligerent mood of the Indians at the time toward the English—was given sanctuary is anyone's guess. Nevertheless, the officer was given the Indian name of "Connestoga" and accepted into the tribe.

Patients often fall in love with their nurses, and Connestoga was no exception. With the old chief's blessings, the white convert married Nocatula.

But the marriage was star-crossed from the beginning. Much ill feeling still existed among certain Indians toward the white man. War chiefs like Dragging Canoe were whipping up frenzied hatred among the tribes, and the new bridegroom was regarded with more than passing suspicion.

One warrior decided that he would solve the problem of the white man himself. Not only did he hate the whites, but he, too, was in love with Nocatula. By ridding himself of his rival, he would kill two birds with one stone.

The jealous man saw his chance one day and plunged a knife deep into Connestoga's chest. Then he fled.

As Connestoga lay dying, Nocatula declared her undying love for her husband. Then she took her own knife and plunged it into her own breast.

The old chief was deeply saddened at the loss of his daughter and son-in-law. Luckily, the murderer had not escaped the village, and when he was returned—and according to the Cherokee right of blood revenge—the old chief killed the man himself.

Then the chief buried his daughter and her husband. In Connestoga's hand he placed an acorn. In his daughter's, he placed a hackberry.

Fed by the bodies beneath the ground, these two seeds grew into healthy trees and thrived for over 150 years. But as all living things do, they eventually died.

Two more trees were planted over the graves to replace them. But then something odd happened. The two substitutes died a short time later for no reason. The legend is told that the spirits of Connestoga and Nocatula rejected the surrogates as unworthy, and killed them both.

Today only stumps of the original oak and hackberry remain, planted over two centuries ago by a sad old Indian chief who wanted to symbolize the everlasting love between his daughter and the white man she loved enough to die for.

THE GHOSTS OF TENNESSEE HIGH

Schools and universities, like theaters, are famous for their resident ghosts. There is something about the eccentric atmosphere of a hall of learning that promotes hauntings. And nearly every one of these citadels can boast at least one ghost.

Here is a tale from one Tennessee high school that has suffered more than its share of hauntings.

Tennessee High School in Bristol not only has one ghost—it has three! All have been seen, or heard, by generations of students and faculty alike.

First there is a young girl dressed in a white evening gown who haunts the old part of the school. The second is an old-time steam locomotive that roars out of the auditorium in the middle of the night, flies down the hallway, and then fades away in the old gym. And the third ghost is that of an athlete killed in an auto accident, whose shade is sometimes seen in the Field House.

Tennessee High School was built in 1939. The original high school was called Fifth Street School.

In the 1970s a new section of Tennessee High was built behind the original building. Then in the early 1980s, the vocational wing and Viking Hall were added.

Frank Maple has occupied a classroom at Tennessee High

School, where he teaches chemistry, for years. He hails from Carter County, where he served as a school principal for two years. Maple has had more than his share of experiences with the ghosts of Tennessee High, and his students have shared many of those adventures with him.

Until a few years ago operettas and plays were performed at Tennessee High School, and Maple was always in the thick of the productions, acting as stage manager. Preparing for a play required students to work on the sets late at night. It was then that weird things happened. Foremost of these was the ghost called "Agnes."

"Agnes is the ghost of a young girl who was supposed to have been killed during class night," Maple told me. "Class night was when juniors were installed as seniors, and the seniors were given a farewell salute from the school. It was always a very formal affair. However, students sometimes threw rowdy parties after the ceremony.

"The next morning, after one of these class nights, they found Agnes dead in the school's swimming pool."

Nowadays Agnes roams the original part of the building— she has never been seen in the new section.

"The hallways in the old part of the building were once tiled," Maple said. "Sound would bounce all around. At night, when walking down the hall, you could hear footsteps behind you. Then you'd turn around and there would be no one there."

One night a young teacher, a cynic when it came to ghosts, was working late in his classroom. All of a sudden he heard locker doors slamming in the hallway. Thinking that a vandal might be afoot, he rushed out of his room. There was no one there.

"He got so excited that he called for backup," Maple laughed.

Agnes is not only heard, she is seen—and her appearances are, as Maple explains them, as regular as clockwork.

"When the chorus was producing an operetta," Maple said, "me and some of the students would be on the auditorium stage until eleven or twelve at night working on the sets. And at twelve midnight, every night, Agnes would come floating down out of the attic entrance and sit on the rail above the clock, swinging her legs back and forth.

"She always wore a long white evening dress—the kind of dress she would have worn during class night. She'd watch the stage for a while, and everyone down there would see her. Then she would turn and begin to walk back to the attic, gradually fading into nothingness as she walked away."

One night Maple's students were working very late on a set. At midnight it suddenly got deathly quiet in the auditorium. The students were still hammering away, and the saws were sawing, but there was no sound—just like a silent movie.

And sure enough, Agnes—"just like clockwork"—floated down out of the attic entrance way and sat on the rail above the auditorium clock, swinging her legs.

Other things happen in the school that have never been explained—at least, logically. So they're connected to Agnes.

Sometimes one half of a fluorescent light will work just fine, and the other half will flicker. "When that happens," Maple said, "we say that Agnes is dancing on the ceiling."

The operettas and plays ceased about five years ago, so there is no reason why students should be in the building late at night anymore. Sightings of Agnes, therefore, have decreased. And the hallways are carpeted now, so her footfalls are not heard anymore.

But custodians have told Maple that they sometimes feel that something is following them in the old part of the building—a presence. They just can't hear the footsteps.

Seeing the ghost of the girl in white does not frighten Maple in the least, he says. But he does admit that being followed in the hallway by something unseen does give him the creeps.

And speaking of hallways...that same hallway where Agnes walks in the night harbors another ghost—this time it's a train!

Once again the clock shows midnight. Maple, whose chemistry lab was once located where the principal's office is now, said he and his students would be working late there. Suddenly he would hear a sound coming from the auditorium—the sound of an old-time steam locomotive coming toward him at top speed.

Then the sound would emerge into the hallway, roar past him, and fade away as it entered the old gymnasium. The sound of the passing train was very loud, Maple said. Even the floor vibrated when the ghost train passed.

Again, due to changes in the school's schedule, students and faculty no longer frequent the building late at night, so the sound is not heard as often as before.

The question is, Where did the ghost train come from? Was there once a mainline track that ran where the hallway is now located, before the school was built?

The third ghost at Tennessee High School, Maple said, is that of a former athlete who was run down by an automobile one night as he was walking home from a ball game. Although this ghost is the least known at the school, several students have reported seeing him while attending games in the Field House.

Maple believes in ghosts, and he believes that odd and unexplained phenomena really do occur within the walls of Tennessee High School. But he is not afraid of the ghosts. And, he said, neither are the students.

"The ghosts have not hurt anyone and have not damaged anything," he said. "And so what if someone might think they're not real?" he added. "The students really enjoy hearing the stories."

And so do the rest of us!

THE GHOSTLY GUN BATTLE

Spectral replays of history are quite common in ghostlore. Nearly every battlefield has its own legend of ghostly armies that regularly clash, especially on anniversaries of a conflict. Gunfire and the screams of the wounded are heard. Sometimes even the pungent odor of powder smoke is detected.

Such a legend exists at Shiloh, where on April 6 and 7, 1862, Confederate troops surprised and nearly defeated General U.S. Grant. The carnage was terrible. The Union suffered 13,000 casualties to the Confederacy's 11,000.

And at Gettysburg, Pennsylvania, 13,000 Confederates under General George E. Pickett charged over a mile across open field to attack Union lines atop Cemetery Ridge. In that terrible battle, only one third of the Southern participants returned to their lines unscathed. And on each anniversary of Pickett's Charge, July 3, 1863, the sound of ghostly battle can be heard echoing across the hills and fields of Gettysburg.

Sudden, violent death is the kind of trauma that often produces ghosts. Here is a story from upper East Tennessee, about a moment of terrible violence that is said to live over and over again.

The Long Island of the Holston River has long been the scene of unsavory episodes. That is because it is a cursed island—cursed by the Cherokee who were forced to abandon this strip of land which is located in what is now the modern city of Kingsport. Human behavior on Long Island sometimes expresses its darkest side.

The Cherokee long regarded Long Island as sacred ground. It was a solemn place where Indians hammered out treaties and held religious ceremonies. It also served as an unassailed sanctuary where no person could be killed—no matter the reason.

In July 1777 the Cherokee and whites parleyed on Long Island. An agreement was reached that required the Indians to forfeit certain portions of land to the whites—including the Cherokee's beloved sacred ground. After the meeting, a disgruntled Indian medicine man was said to have placed a curse on the island so that no white would ever live there in peace again.

Since that time, strange and violent events have occurred on the island.

In *Haints, Witches and Boogers: Tales From Upper East Tennessee*, for instance, I told the story of the horrible shade of a homicidal, club wielding manic who periodically attacks lovers on lonely nights. Furthermore, the shades of long-dead Indians and long-extinguished campfires sometimes appear along the banks of the Holston River.

Another story connected with the island concerns the unearthly echoes of a bloody gun battle that took place there on April 25, 1925, between a notorious fugitive from justice and the police officers that attempted to ambush him.

Kinnie Wagner was wanted in Mississippi for killing a sheriff's deputy. He had claimed the shooting was justified. A friend had given him a watch for safekeeping. But the law accused Kinnie of stealing the watch.

Kinnie claimed that he had been framed by a whiskey-dealing sheriff who had employed him to run moonshine. When the FBI began investigating illegal alcohol operations in the county, Kinnie claimed that the sheriff was afraid that he knew too much and would squeal to the law. He was arrested on the trumped-up charges but escaped from jail in Lucedale.

On Christmas Eve, 1924, the sheriff sent a deputy named McIntosh to recapture him, but the deputy had made the mistake of lying in ambush. Kinnie shot the man dead, then fled back to Virginia.

Kinnie Wagner was born just outside Gate City, Virginia, on February 18, 1903, a son of Charles Monroe and Nannie Wagner. He grew up in the mountains and knew each ridge and hollow like the back of his hand. When he was about seven years old, his father bought him his first gun—a Remington single shot .22.

Faithful practice made Kinnie a crack shot. Folks in Scott County claimed that he could hit anything that he could see. The odd thing about Kinnie's shooting style, however, was that he never sighted his rifle—he always shot from the hip.

In 1919, young Kinnie, longing for adventure, joined the Richard Brothers Circus while the show was playing nearby Clinchport. He hired on as a teamster at only $35 a month because the circus boss thought he was too small to do any heavy work. But Kinnie soon proved that he was the equal of any man.

As one of their attractions, Richard Brothers offered a "Bronc Show" and had a number of cowboys on their payroll. One of the horses, called "Funeral Wagon," was an uncontrollable beast who had never been ridden the full ten seconds. One day the cowboy who always rode Funeral Wagon got too drunk to perform, so young Kinnie was ordered to fill in for him.

The problem was that the spunky lad rode Funeral Wagon for the full ten seconds—and beyond!

Not wanting Funeral Wagon to be tamed, the panicked circus boss signaled Kinnie to take a fall—which he did. Thereafter he was the only one who rode the renegade horse, always abandoning the saddle just before ten seconds was called. Because of his skill as a bronco buster, he became known to audiences as "The Texas Kid."

At the time, circus folk were a rough bunch of people. And since Kinnie was physically smaller than the rest, he was naturally picked on. But he learned to use his fists as well as a pistol. Unfortunately he fell in with the wrong crowd; and when he left the circus, he began running moonshine in Mississippi. This, of course, led to his arrest, the jail break, and the subsequent shootout in which the deputy was killed.

On the lam from the law, Kinnie Wagner was holed up just outside of Gate City, where friends and family hid him. Mississippi offered a $1,000 reward for Kinnie's capture, dead or alive. This temptation whetted the appetite of some local law enforcement officials. They were certain Kinnie was in the area, but they just did not know where.

Then one day the Kingsport police learned that Kinnie planned to meet his sister at the park on Long Island. She was graduating from high school and had not seen her brother for several years.

In spite of warnings by their friends, a daring plan was hatched by four Kingsport policemen and a Sullivan County deputy sheriff. They planned to ambush the fugitive and, obviously, had no intentions of taking him alive. On their way to Long Island, the officers had ordered an undertaker's ambulance be sent to the park to collect Kinnie's body.

Kinnie, his sister, and three female relatives met on Long Island late in the afternoon, oblivious to the plot against them. The officers were already in waiting, well hidden behind some bushes and trees. Although he was thoroughly enjoying his first visit with his sister in years, Kinnie, as usual, was ever alert for trouble. So when he saw a bush shake to his left, he drew his pistol and sprang to his feet.

"The fugitive, probably seeing that he was hemmed in from both sides," reported *The Kingsport News*, "took refuge behind a big sycamore tree and began shooting. [Officer George] Frazier was the first to fall.

"The stranger [Wagner] then turned and fired several shots at [Officer George] Smith who died in his tracks. [He was shot through the heart.]

"When Smith had fallen the fugitive turned his guns on

[Deputy Sheriff Hubert] Webb, who was peering over the overhanging [sic] bank in an effort to get a better shot. Webb fell on the crest of the bank." He had been shot in the face.

Bullets were flying fast and thick. One of them clipped Kinnie's sister's hair while another plowed into the ground beside her foot. His relatives dove for cover while Kinnie lit out across the field, running as fast as he could go.

At the same time, Dewey Nelson of Kingsport was riding by on his horse. Kinnie ran up to him and commandeered his animal, promising to return it later. Then he and the horse plunged across the Holston River, galloped up a steep bank, and disappeared from sight.

When the smoke finally cleared, Webb and Smith were dead, and Frazier was seriously wounded. The undertaker's ambulance was needed after all, but not for the party for which it was originally intended.

The next day the offended editor of *The Kingsport News* angrily wrote, "The tragedy was the most shocking and disastrous one that has ever occurred in or about Kingsport. With ten orphaned children and two newly made widows weeping in their homes, dozens of men of Kingsport and vicinity turned out on the manhunt for the desperado."

Kinnie had returned to the Clinch Mountains, and it is doubtful that the posse would have ever caught up with him. By the time it was formed, Kinnie was in Waycross, Virginia, snuggled up in a haystack.

When the woman who owned the farm came to the barn the next morning, she discovered Kinnie and advised him to surrender—for his own good. He agreed with her and, later that day, turned himself in.

Kinnie went to trial in Blountville, and after thirteen hours of deliberation the jury returned a verdict of guilty. He was sentenced to die in the electric chair.

But he wasn't ready to die, and no jail had been built that could hold him. So Kinnie Wagner escaped and became a fugitive again.

In the meantime, some folks say, every April 13th ghostly gunshots ring out again on the Long Island of the Holston as the spirits of Kinnie Wagner and the law repeat their deadly battle on the very land where, according to the Cherokees, no person could ever be killed.

THE HAUNTED TV STATION

Ghosts in a television station?

Anything is possible in the world of the supernatural, as some of the staff at WATE-TV in Knoxville will tell you. Their station is located in the palatial former home of Major E.C. Camp.

Major Camp, a former soldier in the Union Army who made a fortune in coal and marble, took five years (1885-1890) to build his stately home on Broadway.

When WATE moved into the old house, staff members began hearing mysterious noises in the building that could not be explained away. The noises—including footsteps—mostly occur late at night. There haven't been, however—as far as anyone has told me—any apparitions. But we can't say there never will be.

Perhaps, in the future, viewers may be treated to an unscheduled appearance of Major Camp's shade on the eleven o'clock news. That would be quite a scoop!

UNQUIET GRAVES?

This is one of those thrilling tales about haunted graveyards with an added touch. How would you like to trade places with the young man in this story who was confronted late one night by a giant of a man with a foot-long knife?

At first glance Jobe Cemetery does not look much like a haunted graveyard. And it's also hard to imagine that little Jobe once had the infamous reputation as a "murderin' ground."

In the early part of this century, Jobe was surrounded on three sides by woods. Hidden in the tangle of trees, vines, and underbrush was a fallen sycamore which served as both a table and a bench for railroad hoboes who visited Erwin in Unicoi County. From this "headquarters" the hoboes fanned out into the town during the day, begging for food or money. Some would do odd jobs in exchange for a full belly. Others would steal what they wanted.

At night the hoboes returned to their fallen log to drink rotgut whiskey, get drunk, play cards, and gamble. Drunken men and gambling don't mix, so a friendly game of cards occasionally turned ugly. Knives or pistols were drawn and, invariably, one of the combatants would get badly hurt or even killed.

The ghosts of a hundred murdered men were said to walk

Jobe Cemetery—at least, that's what generations of Erwin children firmly believed.

Jobe offered delicious adventure to Erwin's young. They would sneak down to the graveyard in the middle of the night and hide in the bushes, hoping to get a glimpse of a ghost or even witness a murder.

Periodically the Unicoi County sheriff raided the woods behind Jobe, flushed out whatever hoboes were there, and hauled them off to jail. But this was mainly for show, to demonstrate to nervous Erwinites that the law was ever vigilant.

But the Unicoi County jail was small and the sheriff could only keep a vagrant locked up a short time. Upon release the hobo would be escorted to the city limits with a stern warning that he had better not show up in town again if he knew what was good for him. But, like the periodic roundup of hoboes at Jobe, the warning was as empty as a rain barrel in a drought. All concerned knew the vagrants would quickly return to business as usual.

One of the most feared railroad hoboes was nicknamed "Old Dawg." No one knew his real name. He was called Old Dawg because his deeply lined face and expression closely resembled a bloodhound. His general disposition, however, was more like a bloodhound with rabies.

Legend around the railroad had it that Old Dawg had killed as many as thirteen men in Erwin, mostly in knife fights. Indeed, the sleepy-eyed hobo was said to carry a blade that was at least a foot long. Other hoboes avoided Old Dawg if they possibly could. Anyone getting into a card game with Old Dawg had better lose, if he knew what was good for him!

Old Dawg was also an exceedingly mysterious character. There was no denying he was a hobo. Yet no one had ever seen him riding a train. In fact, no one had ever seen him in any other town except Erwin.

When he first appeared at Jobe, the other hoboes thought he actually lived in town. But the Unicoi County sheriff, who knew everyone in Erwin (as well as the surrounding countryside), had never seen him before. In fact, he had never seen

Old Dawg at all. He had only heard about him from hoboes he jailed.

One night in the 1920s, several local youths decided to visit Jobe to try to see a ghost. About ten o'clock a half-dozen boys gathered on Main Street in front of the cemetery, and they stared nervously at the tombstones reflecting white in the moonlight.

A young man glanced toward the woods. The others knew what he was thinking. Were hoboes there tonight, and would the intruders be pounced upon and murdered? The parent of nearly every child present had warned him—at one time or another—to beware of Jobe after dark.

But the warning only whetted young appetites for high adventure. Every boy there had sneaked past the bedrooms of sleeping parents, because each had promised his friends to be present this night. No self-respecting young man wanted to be called a "yellow coward" by his peers.

A slow freight of loaded coal hoppers rumbled past on the Clinchfield's main line as a cloud drifted in front of the yellow moon. Now it was so dark in the graveyard that a person could hardly see his hand in front of his face.

"Come on," one of the boys said. "Let's get behind that big bush over there."

"I think I need to go home," said an uneasy youngster. "Tomorrow's a school day and I...."

"What's the matter?" a third boy growled. "You scared?"

"N-not me," came the unsteady answer.

Keeping low, the boys ran across dusty Main Street and crouched behind some tall bushes at the edge of the cemetery. One of them, the ringleader, poked his head up over the shrubbery and peered into the darkness.

"See anything?" one nervous boy whispered.

"Not yet," the ringleader answered confidently.

The rest of the boys raised up so they could see better. At the edge of the woods, across the mass of granite tombstones, one of the boys spied a campfire flickering in the woods. "See that firelight?" he whispered.

"Yeah," the ringleader answered. "I wonder what them

hoboes are up to?"

"Up to no good, I'd say," the nervous boy answered. "Let's just hope they stay in the woods where they belong!"

Suddenly a dark figure appeared on the other side of the graveyard beside the woods. Each boy held his breath. One of the hoboes had emerged from the woods and was slowly making his way across the cemetery.

The first thing the boys thought to do was run. But good sense abandoned them as they hunkered behind the bush and watched the lone figure approach.

He was a big man—the biggest that some of them had ever seen. He wore a heavy coat although it was late spring and warm. On his head he wore a huge slouch hat that covered his eyes.

The figure paused.

The ringleader turned to his companion. "Let's get outta here!" he said breathlessly.

"You don't have to tell me twice," was the hasty answer.

All but one boy broke and ran toward Main Street. The remaining lad, the same boy who had suggested that he go home because the next day was a school day, was too frightened to move. Instead he watched the figure continue its glide toward the bush.

Then the moon came out from behind the clouds, and pale yellow light fell on the figure's face. It was Old Dawg!

Old Dawg pointed a burley hand at the quivering lad. His eyes were white in their sockets—no pupils or irises. His mouth was filled with sharp, rotten teeth. His face was covered with blood.

"I kill you!" he said in what was more of a hiss than a voice.

"N-no, sir," the young boy shouted. "Not me you don't!"

The boy tried to run, but to his horror he found that his limbs were paralyzed. He couldn't move! As Old Dawg approached, all the boy could do was look into those horrible blank eyes. He then closed his own and began to pray.

Then the boy felt a rush of cold air that raised goosebumps all over his body. But that was it. Nothing more than the cold.

Still he waited for the death blow to fall. After a moment of silence, he slowly opened his eyes. Then he found he could move his arms and legs. With all the strength left in him he scrambled to his feet and ran away.

Later that night, when the boy finally caught up with his friends near Union Avenue, he told them of what he had seen.

"It was Old Dawg," he said breathlessly. "He stood so close I could have touched him if I wanted to."

"What happened?" the ringleader asked.

"I ran as fast as I could," the timid boy replied.

Another boy piped up. "Daddy told me once that he thought Old Dawg was a booger—a ghost of a murdered hobo that roams Jobe Cemetery in search for victims—his revenge for being murdered."

The timid boy shuddered. "I believe that he is a ghost, too," he said.

The ringleader frowned. "Why?"

"Well," he answered, "As I was running away I looked back. And I could have sworn I saw Old Dawg disappear into thin air!"

THE PHANTOM HORSE

Sometimes supernatural incidents might seem to have natural explanations. And just when we appear to have solved the puzzle, nature throws us a curve and dashes our theories all to pieces. Take, for instance, this chilling case.

The National Fish Hatchery near Erwin in Unicoi County has operated since the early part of the twentieth century. The hatchery raises fat rainbow trout which are later released into Tennessee's rivers and streams.

At one time the hatchery was a major employer in Unicoi County and much larger than it is today. Not only were trout raised there, but also bass. The Clinchfield Railroad even built a spur line into the hatchery. There the fish were loaded onto a special car and toted off to their destination. Today, trucks are used to transport the fish.

The back part of the property has since been turned into a public park complete with swimming pool, picnic areas, baseball fields, and tennis courts. Fishery Park is one of the finest parks in the state and the last place one would expect to find a ghost.

During the hatchery's heyday, a tiny settlement grew up around the complex and was called, understandably enough, Fishery Community. In the years just before World War I a carpenter and blacksmith named Henry Banner lived in the

Fishery Community in a two-story white house with his wife, Dora, and eight children. A ninth child, a son from a former marriage, lived a few miles away in the Rock Creek Community.

Henry and Dora's oldest son, Guard, worked at the hatchery part time. His job was to help feed the legions of fish in the numerous ponds and to do general maintenance work.

Although Guard's story takes place in the late teens, automobiles were still fairly uncommon in Unicoi County. Horses were relied upon to wend their way across the rugged mountain terrain and over rough dirt roads that turned into sticky quagmires when it rained.

One hot summer night Guard quit work and had begun walking home when he heard the unmistakable sound of a horse stomping around and nickering in the darkness. Thinking the horse might have somehow gotten loose from its tether, Guard started moving toward the sound. The noises were coming from the direction of the railroad tracks—the Clinchfield main line to Johnson City.

A little path led through the woods, circled around, then ended at the hatchery. Guard stood silently for a moment and listened. He clearly heard a horse snorting and the sound of its hooves stomping along the hard-packed dirt of the trail. Yes, indeed. There was a horse loose in the woods, all right. Guard set out again in the direction of the sounds.

Fifteen minutes later, and very frustrated, he still hadn't caught up with the horse. The moon was out, bright and full. It was about 10:30 and Guard was getting sleepy.

Maybe I should go home and go to bed, Guard thought to himself. *After all, a loose horse will most likely head for the barn when it gets hungry.*

Then Guard heard a loud sound like something splintering wood. He knew there was a gate at the bottom of the hill—a double gate latched shut by a generous length of heavy chain.

The horse must be trying to kick the gate down so he can get through, Guard thought. *He might be tangled up. Maybe I should go down there and help him out.*

To the right of the railroad tracks is the woods where Guard Banner chased the phantom horse late one night. The Fishery Depot, now torn down, stood nearby. The tracks, once belonging to the Clinchfield Railroad, are now owned by the CSX.

Guard skittered down a steep hill and found the gate. He looked around. Not another living thing was in sight. Guard checked the chain—still latched. And no damage had been done to the gate!

Maybe the horse jumped over. No, the fence was much too high for that.

Then Guard looked at the ground. There in the moonlight he saw a fresh set of horse's hoof prints. They approached the gate on one side, then continued on the other side. The animal that had made them couldn't have jumped the gate, because the prints were much too close to the fence line. It looked as if the horse had walked clean through the gate like a ghost through a solid stone wall!

Guard listened again for noises, but all he heard were chirping crickets and a little breeze rustling through the trees—the usual sounds of the night. Needless to say, the young man was quite shaken.

A few minutes later Guard was inside the small store next to the Clinchfield depot at the Fishery, telling the tale to his friend Jim Whaley. Whaley laughed out loud.

"I've heard that old horse a dozen times myself, and I know you told the truth about it," Whaley said. "And I know lots of others who've heard it too!"

Guard Banner never heard the phantom horse again. But he never forgot the night he tried to follow the sounds it made. He's told the story over and over again to his children and grandchildren. Since then dozens of others have told the same story.

No one knows where the ghostly horse comes from or what it is doing on the path so late at night. No one has ever seen it, but its snorting and footfalls are sometimes heard on moonlit nights, especially when a soft wind blows from the west.

In Unicoi County, as in the rest of mountainous East Tennessee, mysterious and unexplained noises are often heard in the middle of the night—sometimes terrifying sounds that seem to come from nowhere in particular and everywhere in general. Old-timers say that the hollows that crease the mountain ranges act as a natural channel for sound—noises bouncing off the steep walls. When the air is just right a person can sometimes stand at the head of one of these hollows and hear a normal tone of conversation being held a half mile away.

Could this be the reason that Guard Banner heard the sound of the horse that scary night? Well it might be except for one small detail. There wasn't a hollow within a half mile of where he was standing!

THE GHOST OF BOONE LAKE

Ghosts and water seem to go together like tar and feathers. A multitude of phantoms can be found infesting ports, islands, and shorelines. People claim, for example, that the British Isles are the most haunted place in the world. Moreover, large port towns—like Charleston, South Carolina; San Francisco, California; and New Orleans, Louisiana—are famous for their shades.

Ghosts found on the water, itself, are most likely to be objects like ships rather than people. Folklore is filled with tales of ghost ships, like the "Flying Dutchman" or the "Mary Celeste." To sight the "Flying Dutchman" is to bring misfortune.

In Tennessee there is a "ghost ship" of sorts on Boone Lake in Washington County. A speedboat was wrecked there several years ago when it collided with another boat traveling without running lights. One man was killed. And now people along the waterfront claim the noise from the same kind of boat whizzes by them on dark nights. Of course, no craft of any kind is in sight at the time.

THE LIBRARY GHOST

Colleges and universities are probably the most haunted institutions in the world. Anyone who has attended one of these schools can tell you that the pressure of academic life is a force to be reckoned with. And people do odd things under this kind of stress. Some, out of sheer frustration and hopelessness, even take their lives.

At East Tennessee State University in Johnson City there is a story that the oldest dormitory, Carter Hall, contains the shade of an unfortunate student who has roamed the halls for decades—after she killed herself in her room!

Almost every dormitory building and academic hall on ETSU's sprawling campus contains a ghost. There are phantom footfalls in Mathes Hall, a haunted portrait in adjoining Burleson Hall, the ghost of a former college president in Gilbreath Hall, and the ghost of a former custodian in University School—just to name a few.

The most elusive—and maybe the most frightening—ghost on campus seems to be the one who haunts a remote part of the Sherrod Library. For years people have felt uneasy while roaming around the old stacks, but they couldn't explain why. Maybe something unseen was down there with them. Maybe it was their imagination working overtime in the half-light of the big room.

The presence of a ghost in the old stacks was only suspected until one day when a student worker saw the library ghost.

The so-called "old stacks" in the Sherrod Library at East Tennessee State University are tucked away in a nebulous nook behind the brightly lit reference room. Here are kept books that have limited circulation—usually older editions of outdated volumes—but are still valuable in isolated research situations.

The old stacks are dark and shadowy, the shelves squeezed close together in a claustrophobic arrangement. Each level of the old stacks is reached by a narrow, winding staircase that looks like part of the set from a horror movie. Even without the ghost said to lurk in the old stacks, that part of the Sherrod Library can get very spooky.

Students and staff claim an unseen presence is sometimes felt in the bowels of the old stacks, as if someone is looking over their shoulders. The feeling seems to be strongest on the lower floor.

Campus legend identifies the ghost as a former librarian, a no-nonsense matron still jealously guarding her books. Richard Lyons, a former student at ETSU, said every time he went into the old stacks, he could feel someone watching him.

"The feeling wasn't frightening or malevolent," he said. "But it was like someone was concerned—like they thought you were going to steal something and they were watching you to make sure that you didn't."

One student worker in the library, who said she spent a great deal of time in the old stacks, told me this story of her encounter with the ghost. She claims to have actually seen it!

"It was during Christmas break," she began. "Nothing much is happening in the library then. Most of the students are enjoying their vacation, and only a few diehard graduate students use the library. Things are pretty quiet and the library is open on limited hours.

"I decided that I would go down into the old stacks and nose around. I often do that. You never know what kind of treasure you might uncover. I remember once I found an old chronology of music down there—a book that kept me fascinated for weeks.

"Well, I walked down the stairs to the lower level. I hadn't been down there but a few minutes when I got this feeling that someone was behind me. I turned around but didn't see anything.

"I went back to my searching, and a few minutes later I had the same feeling. I turned around again, but nothing was there.

"I'd heard stories about the old stacks being haunted, but I don't believe in ghosts—at least, then I didn't. That place back there is so spooky that I think your mind will conjure up anything. If you think there's a ghost, you'll see a ghost.

"I was in the old stacks about fifteen minutes before I found a book that I wanted to read. I put it under my arm, turned, and began walking toward the staircase. Suddenly I saw a figure descending the stairs.

"At first I thought it was another worker. Well, if it had been another worker, her legs were missing!

"What I saw was the torso of a woman, dressed in an old-fashioned, high-neck maroon dress, gliding down the stairs. My blood ran cold. I could see her face clearly. She had a very stern expression and was wearing old-fashioned glasses. Her hair was tied back in a tight bun.

"The figure stopped at the bottom of the stairs and just floated there for a second or two, looking at me. I was speechless. I couldn't move.

"Then the figure disappeared. I ran up the steps and out of the old stacks as fast as I could. I wasn't going to stay there one more second.

"From then on, I never went into the old stacks again unless someone else was with me!"

A HAUNTED ORGAN

In a certain church in Knox County, there's a wonderful old pipe organ that has sung its glorious song during every regular church service for decades. Not only is the organ a wondrous instrument to hear, it's a sight to behold. Behind the polished oak console, ranks of gleaming pipes tower over a cavernous sanctuary—a sanctuary under whose lofty, towering ceiling worshippers have met for seven generations.

But church services are not the only occasion when the magnificent old instrument rings out. Sometimes, just before the city wakes for another day, the organ's voice is heard; but no one is ever found behind the console. The music is always the same—the strains of a certain Bach choral prelude: "Christ Lay in the Bonds of Death."

Church officials, as well as local police, are curious about the mysterious early morning organist. Sometimes they enter the church in the wee hours, but the playing stops as soon as they pass through the arched doorways. And, as I said, no one is ever found in the darkened organ loft—the church is always empty.

What manner of entity would haunt only the organ of a church? There are no ghosts—that anyone knows of—in other parts of the building. Those who know the history of the organ have a pretty good idea who the ghost is. And many can tell you vivid details about the first "appearance" of the ghost—a memorable occasion that nearly caused a bone-crushing free-for-all.

In the early part of the twentieth century the church vestry voted to appropriate money for the new organ to replace the wheezing specimen that had served faithfully up till then. A builder was contacted and a contract was drawn up and signed. The new organ was designed to be one of the largest in East Tennessee, and it was estimated that the instrument would take several years to build.

The organ builder, quite elderly when the contract was signed, thought this might be the last instrument he would ever construct. He was determined it would be his finest work.

He selected two of his best assistants to help him. Then the builder moved to a house nearby so he could be near the project. He spent many hours inside the church supervising the work.

Over the years the instrument slowly took shape. As soon as the organ became operative, the builder sat for hours at the keyboards, playing his favorite melody—a Bach choral prelude. As he played he would pause for a moment to turn this pipe and adjust that pipe, slowly tuning the instrument to musical perfection.

The builder was plainly obsessed. It became his habit to enter the church at three or four o'clock in the morning, lock all the doors behind him, sit in front of the four ranks of gleaming ivory keys, and play the music of Johann Sebastian Bach until the sun rose. Outside the thick walls of the church, muffled sounds of the organ reached the ears of the occasional passersby, who judged by the sound that they could be hearing the greatest organ in the world.

Three or four years passed, and still the organ was not complete. The vestry approached the builder and inquired as to why the work was progressing so slowly. The builder replied that he wanted to make sure that this organ was the finest ever created—and that took patience. Could he have a little more time to complete the work?

Finally, five years after construction began, the builder declared he could improve the instrument no more. A date was set for the organ's dedication.

A nationally famous organist was engaged to perform on the organ at the dedication service—the pieces he selected would show the organ to its best advantage. The day before the dedication, the man visited the church to try the organ. Of course, the builder was there, beaming proudly. After playing a short fugue on the new instrument, the organist turned to the builder.

"This is without a doubt the finest instrument I've ever played," he said. "I've played them all over the world, but this one is the absolute best!"

"Thank you," the builder replied, but not too humbly. It was not in his nature to be humble, even when it was appropriate.

The organist continued his unbounded praise. "This organ has a richness of tone and clarity that I've never heard before. How did you achieve it?"

"Simple," the builder said. "Of course you're familiar with the Bach choral prelude, 'Christ Lay in the Bonds of Death'?"

"Certainly," the organist grumbled. "I've played it so much during my career that I'm sick and tired of the darn thing!"

The builder smiled condescendingly. "Be that as it may, I took that one work and built my organ around it. I was hoping you'd play it tomorrow at the dedication. I think it would be appropriate."

The organist shook his head. He had an ego, too. "I'm sorry," he said. "As I said, I'm sick and tired of that tune. If I forced myself to play it, I wouldn't be able to do myself or your magnificent instrument justice."

"But," the builder protested, "I was depending...."

"No!" the organist interrupted. "I will not play it, and that's final!" Then, to avoid further argument, he walked out of the church.

That night the elderly organ builder suffered a massive stroke and died. The next morning his landlady found his body and called the police. The sudden tragedy cast a pall over the dedication ceremonies, but the service went ahead as planned.

The church was completely filled with people anxious to

hear the new organ that, up till now, they had only heard through the thick stone walls of the church. The dedication was shaping up to be the cultural event of the year. To great applause the famous organist stepped to the console and, with the appropriate flourish, sat down to play.

The audience hushed. In a moment the church sanctuary was filled with a flood of sound as the performer began his concert with a Bach toccata and fugue. When that was finished, the organist launched into a choral prelude by Johannes Brahms. Then another prelude by Franck. At the end of each selection, the audience applauded wildly. Never had they heard a performance so grand, nor an organ so mighty.

To end the concert the organist would perform the mighty "Toccata and Fugue in D minor" by Johann Sebastian Bach. This was the highlight of the concert and the work everyone was waiting for. If any piece of music would show off the might and power of the new organ, the D minor toccata and fugue would surely do the trick.

All was hushed in the sanctuary as the organist's hands poised over the keys. Suddenly a magnificent sound filled the church...

...but it was not Bach's toccata and fugue.

The organist leaped from the organ bench as if scalded. When he ran from the console the organ continued playing the Bach chorale prelude, "Christ Lay in the Bonds of Death."

"The old man! He's in the organ!" the organist shouted.

The organ was, indeed, producing a powerful sound—all by itself. A woman in the audience screamed. The organist fled the platform, running down the aisles and through the door—closely followed by most of his audience who suddenly realized nothing earthly was producing the music flooding the sanctuary.

As a crowd gathered on the street outside, the organ continued playing inside the empty church. Several hours passed.

About 1:00 a.m. a violent thunderstorm broke over Knox County. That sound, combined with the ghostly playing of

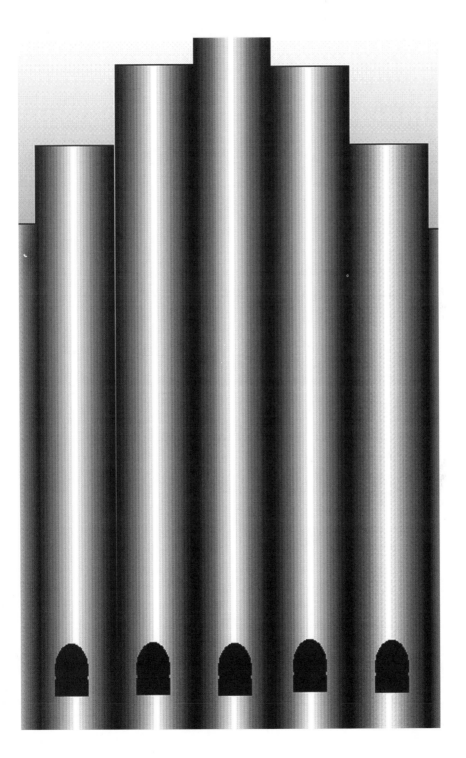

the organ, caused the crowd's collective blood to run cold.

Some members of the crowd wondered what they should do. The police were there of course. But after hearing about the events of the evening, even they were afraid to enter the empty church.

Finally, at about four in the morning, several members of the vestry, well fortified on a local vintage, gathered up enough courage. No sooner did they creep through the door than the organ suddenly stop playing.

Nervously they peered over the polished organ console. Of course, no one was there. The police nervously searched the church from top to bottom but found no one. Then they turned off the lights and left, locking the big front door behind them.

As soon as they stepped into the street they heard maniacal laughter coming from inside the church.

Then once again the magnificent organ began playing again and continued playing the same Bach choral prelude, for two more hours, over and over again, until the sun rose.

FOOTPRINTS IN THE SNOW

A few years ago I accompanied the late Lena Jones, well-known Bristol psychic, as she explored the town cemetery located high on a hill overlooking Jonesborough. Old grave-yards are one of my favorite haunts (if you'll excuse the expression), and I believe a lot can be learned about people of the past by reading epitaphs on tombstones.

Not being a ghost hunter myself, nor claiming any special interest in proving or disproving their existence, I showed my ignorance when I commented that such a spooky place as a cemetery must be filled with ghosts. Lena turned to me like a mother about to correct her child suffering from a serious mis-conception. "There are no ghosts in graveyards," she said firmly. "There is nothing here but dust. The spirits are else-where."

This philosophy, of course, is logical. Just because the body is buried six feet under doesn't mean the spirit remains buried too. If this were true, and if ghosts really do exist, then no one would ever see or hear them. (Such observations, of course, do not stop folks from believing graveyards are home to legions of restless spooks. Remember all those wonderful black and white horror movies set in gothic graveyards?)

But there is also truth in the notion that certain settings—old houses, dark woods and graveyards—sometimes cause the imagination to conjure up ghosts. Landscapes, too, can be eerie. Dark, isolated hollows between mountains, and wild, sparsely populated stretches of real estate can beguile a person into believing that spirits of the dead lurk in every darkened thicket or wild patch of rhododendron.

Here is a case in point.

Fentress County's main claim to fame is being the birthplace of one of Tennessee's most famous sons, Alvin C. York, the highly decorated World War I hero. Born in a remote area known as the Valley of the Three Forks of the Wolf, located near the tiny Cumberland Mountain hamlet of Pall Mall, York fought with the 328th Infantry, 82nd Division, in France.

In the Argonne Forest, on October 8, 1918, York and seventeen men of his detachment were pinned down by machine gun fire while delivering seventy-five German prisoners to the Allied lines. Crouched behind a bush, York, rifle and semiautomatic pistol in hand, was the only soldier in a clear position to fire back at the enemy.

When the smoke finally cleared, he had killed twenty-five German soldiers and had accepted the surrender of the rest. Then York and his men escorted a total of 132 prisoners back to his astonished superiors behind the American lines.

For his heroism York was awarded the Congressional Medal of Honor, the French *Croix de Guerre*, and a host of other military honors. A profile in *The Saturday Evening Post* magazine made him famous nationwide, and offers poured in from manufacturers wishing to have him endorse their products.

Theatrical companies wanted York to appear in vaudeville, and movie companies wanted him for pictures. The offers totaled something around $250,000. But York would have none of it. A conscientious objector when he was drafted into the Army, York did not want to profit personally for killing people in battle—hero or not.

After the war York returned to Fentress County and a hero's welcome. He married his sweetheart, Gracie Williams. Then York spent the rest of his long life quietly promoting education in his neighborhood—an area known for its illiteracy.

The York Grist Mill State Park was established in Fentress County (the county was named for James Fentress, a former Speaker of the Tennessee House of Representatives) to honor his memory. He died in 1964.

Some people say that York's ghost is often seen on the park grounds. But these are only rumors. I have yet to find any firsthand stories of personal encounters with York's ghost. But the hills of Fentress County continue to be wild and remote today—just as they were in York's day. And in areas like this, ghost tales are an essential part of local tradition.

When snow falls on Fentress County, some folks automatically look for fresh footprints that lead for miles through the woods. They are almost never disappointed.

At first glance the footprints look perfectly normal—small and probably belonging to a barefoot child. But barefoot in the snow? Obviously no normal human being could walk shoeless such distances without suffering frostbite, especially a small child. Unless....

Folks tell the story of a little boy, lost and astray in the deep woods around Jamestown. This occurred just after the Civil War. Word had just been received that the boy's father had been killed during the Siege of Petersburg and the body was being shipped back to Cookeville by train. The boy's mother and brothers planned to travel by wagon to meet the train carrying the dead soldier's body.

Just when the train was due to arrive, a violent snowstorm raged over Fentress County. The mother thought it best to leave her three-year-old son at home in the care of his grandmother, an elderly woman well into her eighties. The grandmother had recently become senile, but the mother thought it was better to leave her son there than for him to brave the nasty and dangerous weather.

No one really knows what happened next. Perhaps the old woman fell asleep by the warm fire. Or maybe her mind was wandering so badly that she failed to comprehend what was going on around her. At any rate, the little boy wandered out of the house, without his shoes, and began walking toward Jamestown.

When the mother returned home she discovered her son was missing. By now the storm was winding down, but eight inches of snow lay on the ground. The wind howled through the trees and snow blew into deep drifts.

The frantic mother dispatched her other sons to neighbors' houses to summon help while she began searching the woods for signs of her little boy. Soon the whole neighborhood joined her.

One man discovered a child's tracks in the snow. Shooting off his rifle to attract the other searchers, he began following the imprints. The others quickly joined him, following the tracks and calling the child's name. But there was no answer to the cries, and the tracks in the snow seemed to go on forever.

Later that night another blizzard set in, and what tracks were left were obscured forever. The search was given up and the boy was thought dead, his body lying somewhere under the snow. Two weeks later, when the snow finally melted, another search was launched for the body, but he was still not located.

What had happened to the lad? Had he been kidnapped and taken away. Or was he, as many believe, frozen to death and his body consumed by wild animals? There was plenty of evidence to support the latter theory. The woods in Fentress County, at the time, were filled with wolves and other predators.

One way or the other, the body was never found.

The mother, who had lost both her husband and her youngest child, overcame her grief. The other children grew into manhood.

But the little lost boy would not, and could not, be forgotten. And sometimes, when Fentress County is covered in a blanket of white, the mysterious footprints of a child again mystically appear in the snow, leading nowhere, but traveling on for miles.

When snow covers Fentress County the mysterious footprints of a barefoot child are often seen in the fresh powder. The line of footprints stretches for miles but no one has ever found the source of the tracks. Do the footprints belong to the ghost of a child who was lost in a blizzard over 125 years ago?

THE HAUNTED ROCK

Ghosts associated with small inanimate objects are called "manabees." Whatever the object—be it a gun, a musical instrument, or even a relic from a medieval castle—you might find a ghost cleaved to it. The owner was so attached to the object in life that his ghost continues to cling steadfastly to the object after death.

Manabee hauntings are not a rare phenomenon. In ghostlore they occur all the time. For instance, Guard Banner of Erwin often tells his grandchildren of a gun that was once owned by his father, Henry. The pistol came equipped with its own ghost, a silent apparition of a well-dressed man who accompanied the gun wherever it went. Presumably the man was killed by the gun and his ghost had haunted it ever since.

(For the complete story of "The Hainted Gun," see my book Haints, Witches and Boogers: Tales From Upper East Tennessee.*)*

Here's another manabee tale told to me by a man from Murfreesboro who, in turn, had heard it from his father.

A medieval monastery in Wales had fallen into ruin. A wealthy antiquarian from Murfreesboro thought it might be interesting to possess one of the stones that had served as a foundation for the old building. Arrangements were made with the proper church authorities, and one large rock from the ancient foundation was shipped to the antiquarian's palatial home in Tennessee.

Almost immediately, strange noises were heard in the house—rappings, tappings, footsteps, and the like—the usual poltergeist sounds. Since his house was rather old to begin with, the antiquarian believed, at first, that the noises might have a natural explanation. But they continued night after night, and in the exact same sequence—the heavy footfalls of a line of people walking across the second floor. And an even eerier sound accompanied the footsteps—the sound of men singing in unison. It sounded to the antiquarian like ancient monks chanting a plainsong.

Each time the strange sounds were heard, the man and his servant would climb the ornate staircase to the second floor. They would search from room to room, but they never found anyone. Nor could they find any logical explanation for the noises.

Puzzled—and a little frightened—the man called his parish priest, who came to the house to hear the strange noises for himself.

The priest was noticeably skeptical when he arrived. Ever since the movie *The Exorcist* was released, he had frequently been asked to come to a house and exorcise a supposed ghost lurking within its walls.

The Roman Catholic Church, of course, took a dim view of its clergy striking out on missions of this sort. But, in this particular case, the local priest decided it wise to play some politics. His worried parishioner was a very rich man and a generous contributor to the church coffers. It wouldn't hurt to listen to what the man had to say. Then, if he thought an exorcism was in order, he would contact the proper church authorities.

One night the parish priest sat in the antiquarian's magnificent living room drinking coffee while his excited host animatedly described all the strange noises he had been hearing above him on the second floor. Indeed, even as they talked, odd sounds began drifting down from the second story.

"Hear that?" the old man asked breathlessly. "Doesn't that

sound like footsteps walking across the floor?"

The priest nodded his head. He, indeed, was hearing what sounded like distinct footsteps walking across the wood. But what about the strange singing the man had said he had heard?

The parishioner smiled nervously. "Be patient. It's nearly time."

Then the voices began—at first at a distance, then coming closer. To the priest the voices *really did* sound like a group of men chanting a plainsong. He recognized the tune and it made his blood turn to ice. It was the *Dies Irae*, the twelfth century "Day of Warning."

The voices came closer and closer. The footfalls continued to parade across the wooden floor overhead—the shuffling of dozens of feet in single file. It was a combination of sounds that couldn't possibly have come from a recording.

Now the singing came from all parts of the room at once—from overhead, from beneath the floor, through the walls. Sound surrounded the two men who suddenly found themselves huddling closer.

"It's that infernal foundation stone!" the old man shouted to the priest over the din of voices.

"What foundation stone?"

"The one from the Welsh monastery. The one I had shipped across the ocean as a souvenir."

The priest turned to the frightened old man. "Are you trying to tell me *there is a piece* of a medieval monastery in this house?"

The old man nodded his head.

"No wonder this house is haunted!" the priest shouted, suddenly becoming a firm believer in the old man's story. "There were no more intense religious zealots in the world than ancient monastic orders. As long as you have that rock in your house...." The priest stopped in mid sentence. He could hardly believe what he was saying.

"Do you mean if I get rid of the rock, the ghosts will go away."

"I don't know," he replied hesitantly. "I think so."

The old man cringed in horror as the phantoms of long-dead monks droned a forgotten plainsong—"Day of Wrath"

"Then I've got to get it out of my house before I go crazy!" he shouted as he bolted for the stairs.

Alarmed, the priest tried to run after him. "Wait! Stop! Wait until this is over!"

But it was too late. The old man was already halfway up the stairs. All the time, the singing grew louder and *louder* and LOUDER until....

There was a deafening silence.

The priest stood alone in the living room thinking the old man must have seized the rock and thrown it out the window. What else, after all, could have accounted for the sudden hush? He waited a few minutes and, then, decided to climb the stairs to find his parishioner.

The upstairs hallway was cloaked in shadow. Slowly the priest made his way from room to room, peering in each doorway. Nothing.

Then he heard a voice mumbling from the last room at the end of the hallway. *There he is*, the priest thought to himself. He hurried down the hallway and into the room, but as soon as he passed through the door he froze in his tracks.

The elderly parishioner sat on the floor, a large brown rock cradled in his lap, a monk's habit covering his head and draped over his shoulder. His eyes were wild and he grinned maniacally.

He had picked up the haunted stone in an attempt to rid himself of the infernal haunting. But instead, the demons in the stone had driven him stark raving mad!

The tune of the twelfth century plainsong Dies Irae *(translated as either "Day of Wrath" or "Day of Warning") is quite well known in modern times. Composers have adapted it over the years and incorporated it in their compositions. Its tune, set in a moody minor key, is dark, foreboding, and dramatic. The most famous use was in Hector Berlioz's* Symphonie Fantastique. *More recently the same* Dies Irae *was used as the main theme for the movie* The Shining.

HAUNTED SAM HOUSTON

Some very famous people live very haunted lives. The supernatural frightens them, or they so embrace the unknown that their existence is controlled and directed by its forces.

The English Puritan ruler Oliver Cromwell was said to consult witches and astrologers. Benjamin Franklin was considered by many to be a mystic. In modern times, former First Lady Nancy Reagan used astrology to assist her husband in running the country.

Abraham Lincoln was another person fascinated with the occult. He was known to consult astrologers, to believe in dreams, was visited by ghosts, and hosted seances while residing in the White House.

In the early part of April 1865, Lincoln even had a dream that he believed foretold his own death. He had "awakened" and walked downstairs to the ground floor of the White House. There he encountered a number of people crying in front of a catafalque set in the center of the room.

"Who is dead in the White House?" Lincoln asked cautiously.

"It is the president," came the reply.

Four days later, on April 14, Lincoln was shot by John Wilkes Booth in Ford's Theatre during a performance of the play *Our American Cousin*. The next morning he died in a house across the street.

But according to tradition, Abraham Lincoln still "lives." That would be meet and right for a person who had spent his life dabbling in the supernatural. He would be a prime candidate for ghostly hijinx after his death.

In his book *Ghosts That Walk In Washington*, Hans Holzer wrote:

"It is said that the ghost of Abraham Lincoln walks the halls [of the White House]. Eleanor Roosevelt saw the ghost of Lincoln ambling down the hall. Likewise, former President Harry Truman is supposed to have had an encounter with Lincoln's shade late one night outside his bedroom.

"Lincoln, however, is not a ghost to fear. There is something strangely unintimidating about unexpectedly bumping into the shade of America's greatest humanitarian. Lincoln, when alive, was often visited by the ghost of his son Willie, who died in the White House at age 11....

"The legend about Lincoln's ghost is that it is especially restless on the eve of national calamities."

The ghost of Lincoln is said to also haunt the streets of Springfield, Illinois, floating under the same shroud of melancholy that dogged him when he was alive. As poet Vachel Lindsay wrote during World War I:

"He cannot rest until a spirit dawn
    Shall come;—the shining hope of Europe free:
The league of sober folk, the Workers' Earth,
    Bringing long peace to Corland, Alp and Sea.
It breaks his heart that kings must murder still,
    That all his hours of travail here for men
Seem yet in vain. And who will bring white peace
    That he may sleep upon his hill again?"
                —from *Abraham Lincoln Walks At Midnight*

Tennessee's own Samuel Houston, like Lincoln, was obsessed with the supernatural. A one-term governor of Tennessee, Houston also served as the first president of the new Republic of Texas. After Texas became a state, he served both as its representative to the United States Senate and its governor.

Sam Houston had a reputation for feistiness. A protégé of Andrew Jackson, Houston was considered flamboyant, short-tempered, and heavily addicted to strong drink.

Houston was born on March 2, 1793, in Virginia, the fifth son of Samuel Houston, a major in the Virginia militia. When he was thirteen, his widowed mother moved the family to Blount County, Tennessee, just east of the present town of Maryville.

There young Sam worked in a general store to help with the family finances. But he was dissatisfied with this life and at age fifteen ran away to live with the Cherokee Indians. He remained with them for three years and was adopted into the tribe. There he absorbed a great deal of Indian lore, including their vast store of ghostlore.

When he left the Indians, he taught school for a short while. Then he enlisted in Andrew Jackson's army to fight the Creek Indians. During the Battle of Horseshoe Bend, Houston was gravely wounded but recovered.

In 1817 Houston was detailed to the adjutant's office at Nashville. While there he met Noah Miller Ludlow, late of Samuel Drake's traveling theatrical company, who had come to Nashville with his own troupe of itinerate players. Houston, always with a flair for the dramatic, suggested that Ludlow build and operate a dramatic club in the city. But Ludlow had a tour to complete and set out for New Orleans, Louisiana.

The next year he was back and became stage manager of the Dramatic Club of Nashville. Houston was then working for Judge James Trimble as a legal assistant. The twenty-four-year-old budding lawyer immediately joined the club and snagged roles in a number of plays, including that of a drunken porter in a one-act afterpiece entitled *We Fly By Night*.

Houston considered the latter role as beneath his dignity as an actor. Fully made up in powdered wig and red nose, Houston had to be pleaded with to take the stage. He was afraid of ridicule in such a demeaning part. Finally he consented to make an appearance, but only after he threatened to shoot Ludlow if any of his friends made fun of him afterward.

Fortunately for the impresario, Houston was a hit in the comic role. Afterward, Ludlow wrote that he had never seen a man who had a "keener sense of the ridiculous."

Houston finally hung up his shingle and began practicing law in Lebanon. Jackson never forgot Houston's loyalty and service in the Creek Indian War, and the general used his influence to get his protégé elected first to the Senate, then as governor of Tennessee.

But Houston's hard drinking and carousing caused him both political and personal difficulties. Furthermore, in 1829, just three months after his marriage to Eliza Allen, Houston and his wife experienced what biographer Llerena Friend called "some misunderstanding." At any rate, he delivered his wife back to her parents, claiming that the marriage never existed because it had never been consummated. Shortly thereafter, On April 16, 1829, he resigned as governor and returned to the Cherokee Indians in Arkansas Territory.

The rest of Houston's story belongs to the history of Texas.

Much of Houston's life is regulated to folklore. That is a major problem in researching the lives of larger-than-life characters. They attract legends. That Houston was preoccupied with the supernatural is an established fact. But to what extent was he preoccupied with ghosts and witches, and to what extent did the supernatural rule his life?

Little of Houston's feelings in this area are documented, and I suspect most of the stories fall within the realm of folklore. I talked to several Tennessee historians familiar with the Houston biography, who offered unsubstantiated episodes which they would never utter in a professional capacity. Unfortunately, hard-core historians are like that. But here are a number of tidbits the historians told me (unofficially) about Houston and his beliefs.

The three years that Houston spent with the Cherokee as a boy must have made an indelible impression on his persona. The Cherokee were a spiritual people, and when Houston first joined them as a boy they had not yet totally embraced the white man's ways or religion. Many of their traditions were still firmly in place.

Houston's contemporaries claimed that he followed Cherokee rituals, even after he had left their camps for white man's civilization. He believed in the power of evil spirits. For a time, he even wore a medicine bag around his neck to ward off denizens of the netherworld ("boogers," as the Cherokee sometimes called them).

Houston refused to enter graveyards. He shied away from houses said to be haunted. He even admitted to a friend that he feared that a witch was out to get him, and he had to be careful of what he ate lest the old woman succeed in poisoning him. There is even a rumor that Jackson asked him to accompany his party to the John Bell house (see "The Bell Witch of Tennessee" in this book) but that Houston refused.

Portents ruled Houston's life. One time he was said to have avoided a court date in Nashville because he had had a vivid dream the night before. In the dream he was traveling the road, riding a horse, when he was struck by lightning. Houston awoke the next morning and quickly decided it was too dangerous to travel that day. The court date was missed, which caused great inconvenience to his client, who promptly fired him.

Another time he was said to have foreseen the death of a close friend. Houston tried to warn the man of impending danger but the friend wouldn't listen. The friend later met with a tragic accident and died.

The Cherokee considered Houston a man of great power— even a mystic. They gave him the name of "Raven" and, for all intents and purposes, considered him a bona fide Indian.

In return Houston absorbed a great deal of Indian spirituality. Hence he developed a belief in ghosts, witches, and demons, which, in the Indian world, was appropriate. But once outside that world, his odd beliefs and strange prohibitions sometimes held him at odds with his fellow whites.

The story is told that Houston believed he was being followed by a personal demon who was bent on destroying him. This demon, according to Houston, accompanied him everywhere. It tortured him and his friends. It caused his sometimes erratic behavior. One time he even said he actually saw the demon lurking in the shadows—a great hulk of a creature, taller than a man, with all the bulk of a large bear.

Houston blamed his well-known penchant for the bottle on the influence of this demon. In fact he blamed every one of his failings, throughout his long and eventful life, on the demon. In spite of his many accomplishments, up until the day he died he thought his life had been a complete failure because of the influence of this demon.

Not even Lincoln thought this.

SOMETHING IS TRYING TO GET THROUGH THE FLOOR!

Not too long ago the movie Poltergeist *was released. In it a family was harassed by a number of ghosts, although they didn't know why. Their house shouldn't have been haunted. It was new and located in a modern California subdivision. The shocking answer to the mystery came at the end of the movie when the owner of the house discovered the subdivision was built on top of an old graveyard. In order to save money, the developer had removed the gravestones, but not the graves. And now the restless dead were wandering the earth, seeking revenge for being disturbed.*

Here is a similar story, but one set in Tennessee.

In Clarksville, near an off-ramp of Interstate 24, is a long line of restaurants, motels, gas stations, and a huge mall. These businesses lie in a highly commercialized area known as "The Strip." Only decades before, the ground on which The Strip is located was farmed in corn and tobacco. Then the developers moved in, tore down the farmhouses, and built businesses.

Each farm had a family graveyard where generations of family members were buried. Unfortunately, some of the developers might have been in such a hurry to make way for progress that they moved the tombstones, but not the graves.

One restaurant on The Strip is said to be haunted because

it was built over one of these graveyards. Since the day it opened, the place has been bedeviled by something unseen.

At night, when the customers are gone and the closing crew cleans up for the day, strange noises are sometimes heard. The most prevalent sound is scratching—a sound like something with long fingernails trying to claw its way up through the floor.

Maybe mice were at work in the building. An exterminator was called in. That should have ended the problem. It did not.

Most employees don't mind working in the restaurant alongside two or three other workers. But working alone in the building at night is creepy and a chore to be avoided.

One night Jenny L., a student at a nearby college, was working late in the restaurant. The rest of the closing crew had already gone home.

Jenny, a new employee who had not yet heard stories about the strange sounds, was busily straightening out the stockroom. Suddenly she heard scratching coming from beneath the floor. She stopped and listened.

The noises stopped.

Her first impulse was to blame the odd sounds on her imagination. She resumed working. Again the noises started. She stopped a second time.

Then the scratching sounds moved to the dining portion of the restaurant. *An intruder!* she thought to herself. *And I'm the only one here!*

The only telephone was in the office. She would have to walk through the dining room to reach it.

"I was so terrified I hardly knew what to do," Jenny said later. "Sometimes Clarksville police park on the parking lot with their radar guns, looking for speeders. I looked out the window, but I only saw my little yellow car. This was a weekday, so even the main road was almost empty of traffic."

The scratching noises continued, increasing in volume.

"I had been a runner in high school," she continued, "and had won a number of trophies for the hundred-yard dash. The only thing to do was make a dash for the office—right through the dining room. If I moved fast enough, maybe the intruder would not have enough time to react and I could get into the office and lock the door behind me.

"I heard more noises. They got louder. From where I stood in the storeroom, I could just see the office door. Well, if I waited any longer, I thought, I'd never get up the courage to make a run for it.

"Finally my feet caught up with my panic and I lit out across the dining room, not daring to look to either side. I was afraid of what I would see—maybe someone lunging at me with a gun in their hand.

"I was halfway across the dining room when a dark figure in old-fashioned clothing stepped out in front of me. But it was too late to avoid a collision. And before I knew it I had run clear through the person!

"I stopped just outside the office door, caught my breath, and looked around. The figure was gone—there was absolutely no one at all in the dining room!"

Had Jenny's imagination gone ballistic, or had she really run clear through a ghost?

"Oh, I ran through something all right," she said. "The experience was like running through a freezer. When my body passed through the figure I felt a cold rush—then warmth."

And was she afraid?

"You're going to laugh at this," she answered, "but I was quite relieved when I realized that I had only encountered a ghost and not a human intruder."

THE BELL WITCH OF TENNESSEE

Nearly every person who lives in Robertson County has heard of the Bell Witch. Just ask about her in Springfield, Adams, Cedar Hill, or anywhere in between, and you'll probably get an earful of wild tales about her frightening activities. The Bell Witch, or "Kate" as she is sometimes called, is the county's best known and most notorious citizen.

And she is also the most frightening!

After my book The Infamous Bell Witch of Tennessee *hit the bookstores, I was invited to visit some of the schools in Robertson County to talk to students about the Witch. While there, and on previous expeditions to Robertson County, I got the distinct impression that her influence continued to be felt strongly in the county.*

In every class I visited I asked the same two questions: Have you ever heard of the Bell Witch? Do you believe in her? *I wasn't prepared, however, for the answers I got.*

What really surprised me the most was that the vast majority of children actively acknowledge that the Bell Witch is real. Is this so unusual? I asked myself. Children the world over tend to believe that something horrible lurks in their closets, or an unspeakable ogre lives under the bed. When these creatures emerge at night, who knows what terrible things might happen to the unfortunate resident of the room?

Bogeymen have long resided in the nightmares of the young—they are just called by different names. I have heard of the Slimy Soul-Sucker, the Hook, and even the Purple Grunge. Can we safely assume that the Bell Witch of Tennessee is just another prepubescent horror?

The answer to that question is no. The activities of the Bell Witch are not strictly regulated toward the young. I found that just as many adults can recount firsthand incidents that they readily blame on Kate. And a great many sensible and sober adults, apparently, fear her for what she might do to them.

The Bell Witch is unlike any ghost, bogeyman, booger, terror, or other supernatural entity I've ever heard of. So-called ghost logic is thrown out the window. Kate is an intelligent being capable of both violence and tenderness. She is both hateful and kind. The Witch seems to be consumed with jealousy or softened by compassion. In many respects, the Bell Witch behaves exactly like a normal human being—not a ghost.

The circumstance that makes Kate dangerous is that she is possessed of great power—both physical and intellectual. And the most amazing thing of all is that today, almost 180 years after her alleged departure from Robertson County, her influence in the countryside is still strongly felt.

This command is so pronounced that many clear-thinking folks in Robertson County refuse to deny the existence of the Bell Witch for fear of what might happen to them if they do! Nor do they make fun of her. Apparently Kate doesn't like to be mocked.

Cars belonging to scoffers may stop and never run again. Strange and frightening noises may erupt in their houses. And they might even be visited by the entity herself.

"Paranoia" about the Witch even affects outsiders. When I first visited Robertson County to collect information on the Witch, my attitude was noncommittal—I had no notions about her one way or the other. After all, I'm no ghost hunter. In fact, I'm not even sure that I believe in ghosts. But after listening to seemingly intelligent people relate firsthand accounts of their experiences with the Witch, I found myself being extremely judicious when referring to her—especially in Bell Witch country.

If someone asks me if I believe in the Bell Witch—outside

Robertson County, that is—I tell them I'm not sure if she exists or not. But when I'm in Robertson County and someone asks the same question I answer, "Yes. I believe in her!" (I suppose this apparent hypocrisy is the result of a personal inclination for self-preservation. After all, I do not want my car to quit working. It is a long walk from Adams to Erwin.)

The following is an account of the original Bell Witch haunting.

Adams is an unimposing little country town about forty-five miles north of Nashville and is located at the edge of a grassy steppe area, encompassing part of Kentucky and Tennessee, known as Barren Plains. Today the northern part of Robertson County, where Adams is located beside the flowing waters of Red River, is quiet rolling farmland. Adams, itself, is now little more than a crossing in the road. But almost 180 years ago Adams was a bustling farm community and the location of the most famous (as well as infamous) hauntings in the Volunteer State.

The spirit responsible for the commotion has come down through history as the Bell Witch, and was cast in a different mold than the classic ghost. In fact, the Witch was not a ghost at all, nor was she a witch. (The term "witch" was hung on the entity as a convenience.) What kind of booger the Bell Witch really was was anybody's guess!

The Witch was malevolent, cruel, violent, and often abusive. On the other hand, she—and we will refer to her as "she" from now on, also for the sake of convenience—could be kind, generous, and wise.

Few people ever saw the Witch, but many heard her. She spoke with the host of people who visited the Bell house nightly at the height of the haunting. She argued theology with preachers, and politics with politicians. She gossiped about the doings of Bell neighbors. And to one member of the Bell family in particular she predicted future events that would prove later to be uncannily accurate.

Nowhere in the long history of paranormal activity has

there been anything like the turmoil caused by the infamous Bell Witch of Tennessee. Even today—over 170 years after she supposedly left Robertson County for parts unknown— her influence is still felt in the county and beyond.

John Bell moved with his family to Tennessee from North Carolina in 1804. Over the next decade his farm flourished and his family grew. He was not the largest farmer in Robertson County, but he was prosperous. Bell owned a dozen black slaves, a fine one-and-a-half-story log house, and 1,000 acres of prime land on the banks of Red River.

Bell's trouble began when he entered into a slave deal with a local eccentric named Kate Batts who was thought, by many, to be a witch. He sold her a slave, but she accused him of charging her excessive interest. Bell was accused and found guilty of usury in the Robertson County Circuit Court. A short time later, as a result of his conviction, and at the urging of Mrs. Batts, Bell was excommunicated from the Red River Baptist Church.

Kate Batts then placed a curse on John Bell and "certain members" of his family. In those early days of frontier America, witches' curses were not taken lightly.

Late in 1817 John Bell was walking the north section of his land. In his hand was a musket that he carried in case he came across a fat rabbit that could be added to the stew pot.

Suddenly he saw an animal that he took to be a dog. Stray dogs were a problem in Robertson County. They ran in dangerous packs and often attacked and killed livestock. Bell shouldered his rifle and fired at the animal; but when the smoke cleared, the creature seemed to have disappeared into thin air.

At about the same time, John Bell's daughter, twelve-year-old Betsy, was walking in the family orchard with her brother Drewry. Suddenly they noticed an old woman walking beside them. Betsy turned to speak to her, but the woman vanished.

That night the noises in the house began.

At first came sounds of scratching, wings flapping against the ceiling, or animals fighting. Gulping sounds were heard as well as the smacking of lips. Then the furniture began to move around by itself, and bedclothes were torn off.

The Bells were at a loss to explain the disturbances. John Bell thought it was caused by earthquakes. A son, Richard Williams Bell, described later what it was like in the Bell house during the first months of the haunting.

"A strange noise would be heard in one part of the house. Holding lighted candles, the family would inspect the room, only to discover that the noise had moved elsewhere. Sometimes members of the family would move the furniture around and inspect every nook and cranny, searching for a rat or other animal that might be responsible for the disturbances. Finding nothing, they would be perplexed to hear more noises coming from another part of the house."

In addition to the noises, Richard Williams described how the covers were torn from the beds, accompanied by a noise that sounded like the smacking of lips. No one was able to get any rest until the noises stopped, which was generally in the wee hours of the morning.

John Bell was an intensely private man. He was determined that news of his "family trouble," as he called it, would not leak out into the neighborhood.

Then after a year of disturbances, Bell began suffering what Betsy described as "a nervous condition affecting his tongue and jaw muscles." The ailment caused him much distress when chewing and swallowing.

Convinced his physical problems were being caused by whatever entity infested his house, Bell broke his silence. He called in a friend, James Johnson, to help him determine the cause of the disturbances.

After much praying, Johnson and his wife retired for the night in a room next to Betsy's. It didn't take long for the noises to begin. Something suddenly tore the quilt from the Johnsons' bed. Johnson, no weakling, tried to hang on to the cover, but the quilt was ripped out of his hands.

The next morning Johnson advised John Bell that something unnatural infested his house. He suggested that other friends be called in for help. Since his family's dilemma had gotten totally out of control, Bell readily agreed.

A few nights later the Bells, Johnson, and some of John Bell's friends gathered in the Bell house, trying to decide what to do. Suddenly there came a disembodied voice which seemed to radiate from all directions at once. It was the voice of Johnson, but when everyone turned in his direction it was immediately clear that he wasn't the one speaking.

"Johnson's" voice was repeating—word for word—the prayers uttered by him a few nights before. Then, when it finished, the voice changed into that of a woman.

Once the spirit found a voice, she never shut up again. She loved to talk. Gatherings at the Bell house became a nightly affair. A dozen visitors—only friends of the Bell family at first—waited in an upstairs bedroom for the spirit to speak. They were never disappointed.

If knowledge was a formidable weapon, the spirit's sword cut a wide swath. Her grasp of theology was impeccable—no preacher could win an argument with her. Furthermore she was aware of everything that happened in the neighborhood, including embarrassing incidents that she repeated for all to hear.

In his book, *The Bell Witch: A Mysterious Spirit,* published in 1934, Bell descendant Charles Bailey Bell wrote, "If a man came home drunk, all the neighbors knew it. If he scolded his wife or whipped his children, it was told."

Charles Bailey Bell continued by saying that the spirit's reputation as a busybody, who would tell all, had an unexpected result in and around Adams. Since no one wanted his or her shortcomings known to the neighbors, nearly everyone became a paragon of good behavior.

The nightly gatherings with the spirit at the Bell house were also a time of inquiry into the unknown. The spirit welcomed personal questions from her listeners, although her answers were not always truthful. For instance, she gave many different replies to questions about her origin.

One time she said that she was the restless spirit of an Indian. Another time she said she was the spirit of an early settler of Robertson County who had buried a great deal of treasure and had died before revealing its location. But the answer that shocked everyone, and provided her with the name that she would be known as down through history, came one night in response to a question from the Rev. James Gunn, a frequent visitor to the Bell house.

"I am Kate Batts's witch," the spirit replied to her astonished listeners. And then she confessed that her main mission was to make John Bell's life as miserable as possible and to kill him.

Word of this revelation leaked out almost immediately. For some it was merely affirmation for what they already believed—that eccentric Kate Batts was a witch. Supporters of John Bell shunned Kate Batts, while his detractors thought the prosperous farmer was getting his due for what he supposedly had done to the old woman.

From that time on the spirit that infested the Bell house was known far and wide as the "Bell Witch," or simply "Kate."

The Witch made it clear from the start that she was going to hurt John Bell in any way that she could. If she was really Kate Batts's witch, her motivation was clear. What was not so clear was why she spent so much time abusing his young daughter, Betsy.

Her physical assaults on the young girl were violent and frequent. Witnesses saw Betsy reel from continuous blows to her face, heard the sharp sounds of the slaps, and saw red welts appear on her skin. The Witch pulled her hair and dragged her around the room.

Periodically Betsy was seized with fits where she would appear to be choking, then lie as if dead. But forty-five minutes later she was up and around, no worse for wear.

As Betsy grew older she acquired an ardent young suitor named Joshua Gardner. The Witch apparently hated Josh, but never revealed the reason for her displeasure. She continuously begged Betsy to give the young man up; and when Betsy refused, the Witch attacked her again and again.

The Witch also attacked Betsy's older brother Drewry. Drewry, however, took his punishment quietly. Betsy garnered all the sympathy. After all, she was a little girl and people thought that Drewry, being a man, could better take care of himself.

As word of the notorious Bell Witch spread across the country, news of the haunting reached the ears of General Andrew Jackson. John Bell, Jr., had served as an aide to the famous general at the Battle of New Orleans in 1814. Now Jackson felt the young man and his family needed his help.

Jackson and his entourage reached the Bell home and were welcomed warmly by John Bell. John Jr. was away at the time. In the party was a reputed "witch tamer" Jackson had brought along to dispatch the Witch. As the men waited that night for the Witch's appearance, the witch tamer became increasingly nervous with anticipation. Finally he could take the suspense no longer and dared the spirit to "show" herself.

The Witch replied with taunts and oaths. The witch tamer pointed a pistol, loaded with a silver ball, in the direction of the voice. Suddenly the man sprang from his chair, dropping the pistol and grabbing the seat of his pants. He ran around the room shouting, "I'm being stuck with a thousand pins!"

"I am in front of you. Shoot!" the Witch screamed.

The witch tamer picked up his pistol and tried to fire, but the gun wouldn't discharge. Then the Witch began slapping him. Sounds of the blows echoed through the room. Welts appeared. Then his hands shot to his face.

"It's pulling my nose off!" he shouted.

The witch tamer made a break for the door, followed by the voice of the Witch, who offered all sorts of advice on the proper way to be a witch tamer.

Jackson roared with laughter at the spectacle, but he must also have been shaken by it. Although John Bell invited Jackson and his party to sleep inside on soft beds, the general and his party spent the rest of the night camped out on the Bells' front lawn. Early the next morning they left for Nashville, never to return.

Every night, for nearly three years, the Bell house was

filled with visitors. Hundreds of people rapped at John Bell's door asking to hear the Witch, and none were ever refused. Betsy said later that her father spent a great deal of his fortune feeding and lodging perfect strangers.

His front yard was literally destroyed by milling crowds, by wagons, and by horses. Why he went so far out of his way to be accommodating was never fully understood. Perhaps he felt he was paying penance for past sins. Maybe he really did feel responsible for whatever was happening to him and his family.

Clearly the Witch reveled in all the attention she was receiving. She waxed eloquent on all sorts of topics, and answered most of the questions put to her—even the personal ones. However, the Witch called it quits when she faced a scoffer or someone who was determined to eradicate her from the Bell house.

In the meantime, John Bell was becoming physically weaker, a condition he blamed on the Witch. Finally he was told of a Dr. Mize who lived east of Franklin, Kentucky, thirty-five miles from Adams, and who had a reputation as a magician and conjurer. When John Bell asked James Johnson his opinion of the man, the latter suggested they give the good doctor a try. Everything else they had tried had failed, so what could it hurt?

The problem was to fetch Dr. Mize without the Witch's knowledge. Knowing her dislike for exorcists, there was a real fear that she would fly into a fury and do John Bell or his daughter even more harm.

Johnson suggested that he and Drewry travel to Franklin to fetch Dr. Mize. They would leave for Kentucky at three o'clock in the morning, a time when they were sure the Witch would not be about. That way they could put one over on her.

Both should have known better.

Long before Dr. Mize appeared at the Bell house, the Witch was bragging that she had knowledge of the secret journey. She had followed them after discovering Drewry's absence the next morning and had overtaken the party about twenty miles into their journey.

The Witch had appeared to them on the road, posing as a sick rabbit. Drewry, ever the kindly soul, had gathered the unfortunate animal into his lap, not knowing it was really the Witch in disguise. When the rabbit appeared to feel better, he released it and let it scamper back into the woods.

This the Witch described to her listeners back at the Bell house that night. When Johnson and Drewry returned with Dr. Mize several days later, they confirmed the story about the rabbit.

With Dr. Mize now in the house, the Witch disappeared for a few days. After some hocus pocus with incantations and the mixing of various potions, Dr. Mize confidently declared that the Witch would not return.

Witches, he said, were "shy" of him because his magic was so powerful. The Bells almost believed that the man had been successful until the Witch reappeared one night.

Dr. Mize apparently was unexcited at the disembodied voice of the Witch. She plied him with questions as to his qualifications as a magician, and he was evasive in his answers.

"You have no right to pry into my business," he told the Witch as he brewed a new potion.

"You think you know so much," the Witch taunted. "You have omitted some very important ingredients in your mixture."

"And what is that?"

"If you were a witch doctor you would know how to mix that brew with air so it would become gas. And you wouldn't ask me silly questions!"

"What do you know about this business, anyhow?" the bewildered doctor asked.

"I know you're an old fool who doesn't know what he is doing!" the Witch shouted. Then she exploded with such a string of oaths that Dr. Mize's courage left him and he determined he could do no more good in the house.

He told John Bell he would leave the next morning. Then he confided, "That thing knows more about witchcraft than I do."

The next morning Dr. Mize planned an early start. But the Witch wasn't finished with him yet. The instant he mounted his horse, the animal started bucking and kicking.

"I'll make your horse go," the Witch cackled. "In fact, I'll go with you all the way home!"

With that the horse bolted from the house, kicking and snorting, with Dr. Mize hanging on to the animal's mane for all he was worth. The horse and rider disappeared from sight.

The Witch was as good as her word. That night she returned to the house and told everyone about Dr. Mize's headlong rush to Franklin and about the tricks she had played on him along the way.

Up to this point, some people thought they had seen the Bell Witch in the flesh only as a dog or a rabbit. But Betsy once thought she had seen her in the form of an old woman swinging from the branch of a tree. And on the first day of the haunting, both Betsy and Drewry thought they had seen her as an old woman walking beside them in the family orchard. But no one could actually prove they had seen her, much less touched her.

John and Calvin Johnson were brothers who had spent much time in the Bell house talking to the Witch. By playing politics—the Witch was highly susceptible to flattery—they had gained favor with the entity.

Both brothers had witnessed the Witch's physical attacks on others. Both thought the blows delivered sounded like slaps, and the red imprint of five fingers was often seen on the victims' faces.

Calvin, especially, was curious about the Witch's true form, so he proposed that the entity allow him to touch her. At first the Witch refused, but Calvin's persistence won out. The Witch agreed to the experiment only if Calvin promised not to attempt to grasp or hold the hand that was laid on his.

Readily agreeing to the conditions, Calvin waited nervously for something to happen. An instant later he felt pressure on the back of his hand. He said later it felt feminine, "soft and delicate like the hand of a lady." It was hard to imagine that so soft a hand could raise welts on the face of a grown man!

During the haunting, John Bell's oldest son, John Jr., was strangely detached from the proceedings. Certainly he had been present during the assaults on his sister Betsy. And he could not help but notice the effect the Witch was having on his father. Yet he followed a policy of noninterference. Why?

Years later he confessed to his son Dr. Joel Thomas Bell that all the time he had been engaged in private conversations with the witch. John Jr., unlike others in his family, took no guff from the Witch. He told her in no uncertain terms what he thought of her and her behavior. For this the Witch respected him and treated him as an "equal."

When anyone else asked questions, the Witch gave conflicting answers. But to John Jr. she professed to tell only the truth. As a result, John Jr. was the only person to whom the Witch would predict future events. And, in retrospect, her predictions proved uncannily accurate.

Here are some of the Witch's predictions, in her own words, told to John Jr.:

• **The Monroe Doctrine**. "In your country, John, you have a President [James Monroe] who is earnestly looking after the welfare of his fellow citizens. He desires protection of the United States from European aggression. Before his administration is over his endeavors will place the Americas in a position of security." (The Monroe Doctrine, which declared the Western Hemisphere off limits for colonialization by European powers, was delivered to Congress on December 2, 1823.)

• **The Civil War, the capture of New Orleans by David Farragut, and the death of John Bell, Jr.** "There will be another battle at New Orleans in the war spoken of last night. The city will be captured by a Tennessean. He is an officer in the U.S. Navy now, but he will be on the other side. This fight at New Orleans will determine you to go into the army against the North, but you will not realize your decision. You will depart from this world just after the battle at the city in which you've felt so interested." (New Orleans was captured on April 25, 1862. John Jr. died from pneumonia on May 8!)

• **World War I**. "The United States will have wars, no doubt in your lifetime. But with the exception of the one which will result in freedom for the Negroes, these will not be serious. That is, until a great war which will likely involve nearly the whole world.

"The United States, at that time, will have become one of the world's greatest nations. Therefore it will be drawn into this terrible struggle.

"Millions of men will be killed, countries left in financial straits, and years of suffering invade every nation."

• **World War II**. "For some time after this great war [WWI] there will be threats and signs of another great upheaval which, if it comes, will be far more devastating and fearful in character than the one the world thought too terrible for the mind to grasp."

In addition to all of this, the Witch also hinted at the end of the world.

The Witch had never denied that she was out to get John Bell any way that she could. During the four years of the haunting, John Bell became increasingly weak. His body was frequently racked with mysterious afflictions that forced him to take to his bed.

One morning, in the fall of 1820, he and Drewry were walking toward the pigsty when both shoes flew off his feet. He replaced the shoes, and his son retied them in double knots. Seconds later the same thing happened. John Bell, discouraged and depressed, remarked that the Witch was slowly killing him and that he would soon die.

Then on December 19, returning to the house after feeding the stock, John Jr. and Drewry found their father sprawled unconscious on the floor. All attempts to revive him failed. Dr. George Hopson of Port Royal was called in.

When Dr. Hopson arrived, he asked John Jr. what kind of medicine he had been giving his father. John Jr. walked to the cabinet to show Dr. Hopson the three medicines, but the bottles were gone. In their place was a single bottle filled with evil-smelling, brown liquid. John Jr. had never seen the bottle before.

Suddenly the voice of the Witch echoed through the house. "He will never get up," she shouted. "I did it! I gave him a dose from the vial. Now he will die! He'll never get up again!"

John Jr. took a straw and dipped it in the bottle. Then he drew the straw over a cat's tongue. The animal immediately went into convulsions and died. Then John Jr. angrily threw the bottle into the fire. A tongue of blue flame shot up the chimney.

John Bell lingered near death for almost a day while the Witch screamed and shouted at him, loudly issuing taunts and curses. Finally, early the next morning, the old patriarch of the Bell family died.

During the funeral—one of the largest in Robertson County's history—the Witch continued maligning John Bell's character. Then she entertained the mourners with bawdy songs, continuing the raucous concert until the last spadeful of earth was shoveled over the casket.

With the death of John Bell there was fear that the Witch would redirect the bulk of her wrath toward Betsy. But such was not the case—at least not right away. After the funeral, little was heard from the Witch The next spring, however, all that changed.

Shortly after her father died, Betsy Bell became engaged to Joshua Gardner. One spring day in 1821, Betsy and Josh, along with a number of other young couples, were picnicking and fishing on the banks of Red River. Suddenly the voice of the Witch rang out, "Betsy Bell. Do not marry Joshua Gardner. Betsy Bell. Do not marry Joshua Gardner." The words were repeated a number of times before the voice faded away to nothing.

Everyone was quite shaken by the experience, but none more so than Betsy. She had believed the Witch had finally left them.

That night, over Josh's protests, Betsy broke off the engagement. She was afraid that the Witch would make the rest of their lives miserable, and she didn't want to subject Josh to any more of the Witch's evil shenanigans.

A short time later the Witch's voice was heard inside the house. "I am going," she said. "But I will return in seven years."

Then a ball of smoke shot up the chimney and she was heard from no more—for a while.

Lucy Bell continued living in the house with several of her sons. Betsy married her school teacher, Richard Powell. John Jr. moved to another house on the Bell farm.

In 1828 the Witch returned. But this time she spent most of the visit with John Jr. This second haunting consisted mostly of conversations between John Jr. and the Witch. She caused no mischief the second time around.

A short time later she disappeared again, promising to return to the Bell family in 107 years (about 1935). Of course everyone expected the Witch to fulfill her promise. Charles Bailey Bell, grandson of John Bell, had published his book, *The Bell Witch: A Mysterious Spirit*, the preceding year. The Bell descendants braced for the Witch's return but...

It never came.

Some people in Robertson County do not believe that the Witch ever left the vicinity. They point to the hundreds of odd events—ghost lights, unexplained accidents, every unexplained tragedy—that they can blame on the Witch.

A local cave is believed to be the present-day home of the Witch. The current owners of the Bell Witch Cave claim it is the scene of numerous mysterious and unexplained happenings.

Is the Bell Witch really "alive" and well in Robertson County? Well, there are many there who would not dispute the possibility—that is, if they know what's good for them!

Adams as it is today, a sleepy little community forgotten by time. However, in the early part of the nineteenth century, Adams was a center of commerce.

Red River was one of the major transportation arteries when the Bell Witch haunted John Bell's family. Her voice was often heard along its banks.

This obelisk stands in the middle of the Bellwood Cemetery in Adams, and bears the genealogy of the Bell family. Some of the Bell descendants are buried in Bellwood; but the others, including John Bell and his wife Lucy, are buried in the little family plot on the farm, about a mile away. The body of Betsy Bell Powell is buried in Panola County, Mississippi. The Witch, however, is said to be alive and well and living in Robertson County!

THE GHOST OF PORT ROYAL

There is something about river towns that attracts ghosts. Memphis, for example, has more than its share of apparitions floating around the waterfront.

Small river towns (especially of the historic variety) also have their share of ghosts. Kingsport's old waterfront on the Holston River, for example, boasts the specter of an accident victim who directs traffic along foggy River Port Road.

Here is a firsthand account of the spectral doings in another port town, this one in Middle Tennessee.

At one time Red River was one of the major waterways in north central Tennessee—the gateway to the Ohio and Mississippi Rivers—and the town of Port Royal was a main shipping point for flatboats laden with cargo bound for New Orleans. Today Tennessee Valley Authority flood control projects have reduced Red River to a trickle of its former self, and Port Royal has been saved from being a ghost town by being turned into a park by the State of Tennessee.

The Port Royal Historic Area skirts both sides of Red River, at the point where Sulphur Fork Creek spills into it. The confluence of the two rivers provided enough depth and width, in the early 1870s, to ship cargo by flatboat. Furthermore, regular steamboat service reached Port Royal in 1879, and goods could be shipped to market faster, cheaper, and more efficiently. But Port Royal's prominence as a river town was short-lived with the improvement of roads and other means of transport.

In the early years, being such a busy port, Port Royal was a thriving community with a population of several hundred. There was even a Masonic Order there, organized as early as 1812.

In 1859 the Masonic Lodge building was built at the crossroads of the Port Royal and Clarksville/Springfield Roads. The building was also used, at various times, as a doctor's office, general store, and post office. Masonic Lodge meetings were held on the second floor. Today the old building, renovated in 1979, is utilized as the ranger station and museum for Port Royal Historical Area.

Shortly after renovation, the first ranger moved into living quarters on the second floor of the building. That is when it became apparent that the old Masonic hall was haunted!

Today Mark Swann is the ranger in charge. He is the second ranger to live in the old structure, and did so up until 1992. He and his wife also had more than their share of experiences with the ghost(s) of Port Royal.

"We would come home at night and find that all the furniture was moved around," he told me. "Then I'd be sitting upstairs and we'd hear noises downstairs where construction of the office and museum were taking place. I'd go down and check, but would find nothing."

Swann added that he and his wife would be eating dinner and hear footsteps coming up the stairs. Nothing was found on the staircase either!

"I thought at first that someone was playing a trick on me," he said. "I changed all the locks, but when I came home the furniture still would all be moved around, and the mysterious noises continued unabated."

Then Swann and his wife experienced the most chilling phenomenon of all. While lying in bed, they felt something unseen sit beside them.

"You could feel the bed kind of sink down. Like I said, we never saw anything. But the feeling would tend to wake you

The Masonic Hall at Port Royal was built in 1859, and is now a ranger station at Port Royal Historical Site. Windows on the second floor mark the former residence of the park ranger. Here the ghost of Willie Woodridge moved around furniture and created disturbances. The ghost of his mother is often seen on the front porch of the building, rocking away in her rocking chair.

up." Swann also noted that the bed-sitting episodes always happened at four o'clock in the morning!

He said that his wife became nervous living in the old building, and she would experience the same things at night as her husband did when he was away on business. Their overnight guests reported similar experiences.

Just who was the ghost of the Masonic Lodge? Naturally Swann was curious as to its identity. The same kind of things had occurred in the building when the first park ranger lived there—furniture moving around and phantom footfalls ascending the staircase.

Furthermore, people would drive by the building at night and spy a little old lady on the front porch, sitting in a rocking chair. But when they reversed direction and checked again, she would be gone. Maybe this was the ghost causing all the problems. The problem was that no one had any idea who the little old lady was. Was this the ghost? Or was there another?

Then in 1986 a student from Austin Peay State University, in Clarksville, came to Port Royal to do research. She was the one who discovered the possible identity of the ghost.

In 1903 a 200-foot bridge was under construction across Red River. Up to then, fords and ferries were used to cross the river because the last bridge, built just before the War Between The States, had been swept away in the Great Flood of 1866.

On December 7, the false supporting timbers under the bridge were being removed, and workers on top were warned to evacuate just in case. However, a few elected to stay on.

Suddenly without warning there was an earsplitting roar and great tearing of metal as the new span plunged into the chilly waters of Red River. Of the three workers on the bridge, two had broken bones while the third walked away from the accident uninjured.

A fourth person, however, was gravely injured. The real tragedy was that young Willie Woodridge of Port Royal was not even a bridge workman. He had been on the bridge only as an observer.

Woodridge's broken body was carried to the doctor's office, located on the second floor of the Masonic hall. He died there at four o'clock in the morning—the same time that Swann said he was awakened by someone sitting on the bed!

If the haunting on the second floor of the old Masonic hall has been explained, there still remains the question of the little old lady in the rocking chair. "Oh, that's an easy one," said one of my Springfield friends (a bottomless well of local folklore) who is familiar with the haunting. "The ghost of the woman is Mrs. Woodridge, Willie's mother.

"The way I heard the story.... When she learned of her son's death she rushed over to the doctor's office as fast as she could. The old lady had barely gotten up on the front porch of the building before she dropped dead of a heart attack!"

Funny, isn't it—how historical precedents for some hauntings sometimes naturally fall into place and make the entire affair plausible.

GHOST LIGHTS OF THE CUMBERLANDS

Many people are familiar with North Carolina's so-called "Brown Mountain Lights," possibly the most famous ghost lights in the world. These flitter around Brown Mountain, just off the Blue Ridge Parkway, like fireflies. Even though they can be clearly seen by observers standing by the roadway, they disappear when one approaches the mountains.

Ghost lights are a common phenomenon and can occur almost anywhere. Railroad tracks—especially abandoned routes—often have ghost lights attached to them. In Robertson County, ghost lights around the little town of Adams are associated with the Bell Witch of Tennessee.

Here is a tale of ghost lights said to appear along one of Tennessee's "wild" rivers and even travel across part of Interstate 40.

The Cumberland Mountains are a part of the Appalachian chain. They slash across Tennessee between Knoxville and Nashville, then northward into Kentucky, where they form that state's boundary with Virginia.

As mountain ranges go, the Cumberlands (or as some geographers call the rugged area, the Cumberland Plateau) are not very high—only 2,000-3,000 feet above sea level. But a complex series of streams and rivers has carved valleys and gorges in the mountains that are, especially on the western slope, as deep as a thousand feet.

The soil is not very fertile in the Cumberlands, so there were not many farms in the area by the end of the nineteenth century. But wildlife was plentiful, and a number of men still made a living like their ancestors, by hunting and trapping.

A major producer of gorges is the Obed River, a wild and winding stream. Today Interstate 40 crosses the Obed only a few yards from the spot where once a horrible triple killing took place.

Three mysterious balls of light are frequently seen gliding over the river valley, sometimes crossing I-40, and then disappearing into the river on the other side. (This is the only instance of a ghost light crossing a major highway that I've ever heard of in Tennessee, and it must be most unnerving to motorists.) These lights are said to be the souls of three men—a trapper and the two men who murdered him. A local story speculates on what happened that terrible night nearly a century ago.

Joel T. of Nashville had heard the story of the ghost lights for years, first from his father, then from an adventurous friend who suggested the pair travel to the gorge one night to see the phenomenon for themselves.

Toward the last of October the Cumberlands are alive with color. Days, for the most part, are warm and nights are crisp. This is the time when the lights are best seen.

Joel told me it was on such a night that he and his friend parked their car at a nearby rest area, walked across the highway, and skittered down a steep embankment into the valley of the Obed. According to the legend, three balls of light should appear just after dark.

The men heard cars and trucks crossing over the bridge above them. The whooshing nearly drowned the gurgling of the river flowing next to them.

"I think the cabin where the murders took place was close to the river," Joel's companion said, pointing to a little clearing. "Let's walk down and see if any part of it is left."

Joel agreed that would be a good idea. So the men began

picking their way along the river bank.

Joel reran the story in his mind. A trapper had lived alone on the bank of the Obed River about the turn of the twentieth century. This was a time when animal pelts still had some market value and a man could make a living by trapping.

The trapper would collect his pelts throughout the year—but mainly in the fall because that was when the coats of the animals had thickened for the winter. Then he'd travel to Crossville to sell the cured pelts to a trader. The pelts would then be shipped to New York, or some other large city, to be sewn into coats, stoles, and muffs.

The trapper had large amounts of cash only a small part of the year—just after his sale. He'd stash his money somewhere in his cabin. Then he'd live off it until it was time for the next year's sale.

Two drifters had heard about the trapper and his money from a local man. The three of them had gotten drunk on rotgut, and the whiskey had loosened the local man's tongue. Later that night the pair of drifters hiked to the cabin with robbery on their minds. It was December—in fact, several days before Christmas. The air was cold and a skiff of snow lay on the ground.

When they arrived the pair hunkered down in the bushes and watched the cabin for signs of life. No light shone through the window and they assumed the trapper was fast asleep.

Silently they advanced. When they reached the cabin door their plan was to knock it down, rush inside, and quickly overcome its occupant. They would steal his money, then kill him so he couldn't tell the authorities about the robbery.

The two drifters heard heavy snoring coming from inside the darkened cabin. One of the men pulled a jackknife from his pocket and opened it. Then he nodded readiness to his companion. The cabin door was old and weathered, so it broke in two pieces when the men rammed through it. Inside, a kerosene lantern burned on a very low flame. The trapper leaped out of bed but was too groggy for his defense to be of much use.

One of the intruders grabbed the trapper in a choke hold. The other man held the knife to his throat.

"Where's your money?" the man wielding the knife demanded.

"Ain't got no money," the trapper replied.

"We know that you do," the intruder shot back. "Give us your money or die!"

The trapper was no fool. If he handed over his cash, he was a dead man anyway. He thought he might be able to bluff.

"All right," the trapper said. "I'll show you where it is. Let me go."

"Nothin' doin'," the man with the knife said.

The trapper had to think fast. "If you don't let go," he said, "I won't be able to get to my cash box."

"Just tell us where it is."

"I can't. I'm the only one who can get it. You're gonna have to let me go."

The two intruders glanced at each other, wondering what to do next. Finally the second man loosed his grip slightly on the trapper's throat. "Okay," he said. "But if you try anything cute, you're dead. Understand?"

"Yeah," the trapper answered grimly.

But the second that he was released, the trapper dove into the man holding the knife and both tumbled to the floor. The knife skittered under the bed.

The second man jumped on top of the combatants, and all three rolled around the floor, arms and legs flailing in every direction. One set of legs hit the small table on which the kerosene lantern was perched, sending everything crashing to the floor. The glass fuel well shattered into a thousand pieces, and the burning kerosene spewed in all directions.

The bed, with its straw mattress, burst into flames. The headboard caught fire. Smoke enveloped the aggressors. The fire was out of control!

Suddenly a knife came out of nowhere and was plunged deep into the chest of the trapper. Then again.... And again....

The second man scrambled to his feet and saw the fire

around him was quickly consuming the cabin. "We gotta find that money and get out of here before we both burn up," he shouted to his partner.

"I think we ought to forget the money and just get outta here," his terrified partner shot back. He started toward the door, which was masked in a solid sheet of flame.

Suddenly a burning tongue of fire shot through the cabin, setting both men's clothes and hair on fire. Frantically they tried to beat out the flames, but it was too late.

The next morning three blackened skeletons were found in the smoldering ashes of the cabin. Robbers and victim had perished together in the flames.

"Look here," Joel's friend said as he pulled away some thick vines. The beam of his flashlight played on some stones half buried in the dirt. "These don't look like they belong here. And what's this black stuff all over the top of them?"

"Maybe ashes or soot," Joel said as he peered over his friend's shoulder. "I'll bet this is part of the cabin's foundation."

"I wonder whether the trapper's money box was ever found."

"I've never heard of such."

Then Joel stood up and looked toward the I-40 bridge. "It's gotta be nearly nine o'clock. I don't think those ghost lights are going to show up tonight."

His friend readily agreed with him and the two men began making their way back to the bridge. Joel looked back over his shoulder toward the old cabin's foundation. He stopped dead in his tracks. Nervously he tapped his friend's shoulder and he, too, turned his attention toward the old cabin site.

Three mysterious balls of light slowly rose from the foundation and began gliding over the little valley. One of the light balls was much larger than the other two, all three had a bluish cast, and each emitted a curious sputtering sound—like the live end of a dangling electric wire.

The lights were only a few feet from the astounded men

when they suddenly changed direction, gliding out over the Obed River. The lights changed direction a second time and continued upriver. Then they coasted under the bridge and disappeared on the other side.

For a long time neither man said anything. They had heard about the lights all their lives, but to actually see them was something else again.

A cold chill encased both.

"I wonder where the lights went to," Joel's friend said shakily.

"Danged if I know," Joel replied. "But I've had enough of the supernatural tonight. All I want to do is get into the car and go home."

"I've never been back to the cabin site since that night," Joel told me. "And I haven't told anyone about my experience there—that is, until now." He thought for a moment. "And there's something else....

"After we started the car and were on our way back to Nashville, I looked in the rearview mirror and saw all three light balls behind the car. I told my friend, so he pulled the car onto the berm. Then we got out.

"Sure enough. The balls of light were there—hovering just a few feet above the road's surface. There was almost no traffic on I-40 at the time—at least not westbound.

"The lights bobbed up and down for a moment or two. Then they turned and glided to the edge of the road and disappeared over the side of the bridge.

"I looked at my friend and said, 'Are you thinking what I'm thinking?'

"'I think so,' he answered. 'If I didn't know any better, I could swear those ghost lights were saying goodbye.'

"And probably 'good riddance'!"

SOMETHING HORRIBLE
IS PEERING IN THE WINDOW

Do we ever get over our childhood fears and finally believe, without a shadow of a doubt, that no monsters are lurking under our beds or in our closets? Or can we really believe that no horrible creatures hide in the bushes just outside our bedroom windows, waiting to spring on a sleeper at the first opportunity?

A successful career woman from Tullahoma, who we will call Tina Brandt, was able to hold her own in the rough and tumble world of male-dominated business. Her mind was like a steel trap, able to grasp even the most subtle particular of a complicated business deal. On the surface she seemed afraid of nothing.

But nighttime these days are another matter for Tina. As a child she was afraid of the dark. Little Tina believed a monster of gigantic proportions hid in her closet, and she slept with all the lights on in her room.

But as she grew, the fear subsided—as it does for most of us. Then came that terrible night several years ago when she awoke from a sound sleep.

Tina Brandt had just experienced a frustrating day. Beginning at 7:30, she had been embroiled in a tricky corporate maneuver that could have spelled the end of her company had she made even the slightest mistake.

Missing lunch had caused her blood sugar to plunge, so she felt like death warmed over by the time she dragged herself through the door of her split level house, located in a local subdivision. Her spartan supper consisted of leftover spaghetti and some soggy garlic bread. The whole meal tasted stale, but she was just too tired to fix something more desirable.

To relax and wind down she watched the late news on television, then took a long hot shower. It was nearly midnight when Tina finally crawled into bed. As she joked later, she was so tired that when she turned out the light, she was fast asleep before the room was dark.

But it was not a peaceful sleep that Tina would enjoy that night—rather, it was fitful and restless. By 2:00 a.m. she was sitting on the side of her bed, her weary head in her hands, unable to go back to sleep. She thought about watching an early morning movie on TNT—a western that she had wanted to see.

After raiding the refrigerator for a bowl of canned peaches, she flopped down in her easy chair and turned on the television. The movie had already been running a half hour, but that was all right. Tina couldn't remember a time when she had watched a movie all the way through anyway.

The room was dark, the bluish glow of the television screen providing the only light. Outside, a misty rain had begun to fall but was slowly increasing into a steady downpour. Occasionally a flash of lightning filled the sky.

Tina became tired again. She considered going back to bed, but the chair in which she was slouched was much too comfortable. She had already lost interest in the TV program. Her eyelids became heavy, her mind clouded, and she began drifting off into sleep.

Then she was snapped awake by a steady tapping at her window. Nothing was there. She got out of the chair, walked to the front door, and opened it. The cloudy night made it seem darker than usual outside, but the street lights illuminated the immediate area. Nothing was stirring.

It must have been my imagination, she thought.

Tina closed the door and returned to the living room. She switched off the TV and prepared to return to bed. Again she heard the tapping. She turned. Still she saw nothing at the window—just the dark and the rain splattering against the glass. She was perplexed. She had heard something.

Needless to say Tina was getting nervous. She was alone in the house and considered calling 911 for help, but her house was located in what was considered a "safe" neighborhood. There had been no trouble around there before. Why call 911, have the police come to her house, and then look foolish when they found nothing there?

The tapping was heard again. Tina nervously checked the front door to make certain it was locked. Then, just in case, she removed a .38 police special from her cupboard and placed it on the nightstand next to the bed. She crawled under the covers and turned out the light.

She lay in the darkness for a long time, eyes open, ears tuned for the slightest sound. But she heard and saw nothing except for an occasional flash of lightning and a dull roll of thunder.

Maybe it really was my imagination, she thought to herself. *The rain can play strange tricks. Maybe I just heard rain dripping into a metal drain. That would make a tapping sound.*

She glanced at the clock. Two-thirty. I've got to get some sleep. I have a big day tomorrow.

Just as Tina was closing her eyes she heard the steady tapping again—this time coming from her bedroom window. She opened her eyes just in time to see a pair of glowing eyes peering in at her from the outside.

Tina tried to turn over and reach for the gun on the night stand but, to her horror, found she couldn't move! She could only stare in wide-eyed terror at the faceless apparition peering in from outside her window.

The glowing eyes stood still, unblinking, watching her. Then they gradually came closer. Tina realized they were passing right through the window pane—just as if it weren't there. She opened her mouth to scream but nothing would come out.

When the eyes were only four feet from her own, they stopped and hung silently in midair. They seemed to be studying her, taking their time, scrutinizing her every feature.

What do they want? her mind screamed in a panic. *Oh, please, don't hurt me!*

The glowing eyes then began to float toward the ceiling. Since Tina could not move her head, they quickly moved out of her field of vision, but she instinctively knew they were still there—somewhere above the bed, watching her. The next time she saw the eyes, they were drifting backwards toward the window.

Maybe they're going to leave now, Tina thought. *Lord, I hope so. I can't take any more of this.*

The glowing eyes slowly descended—all the time watching Tina as she lay helpless in her bed. Then there was a room-jarring bang. Tina picked herself up off her bedroom floor, where she had been thrown by the concussion.

When she wobbled to her feet and looked again, the eyes were gone!

Lightning lit up the world outside her window, and thunder rumbled across the heavens. She was alone.

Considerably shaken, Tina sat on the side of the bed. Any moment she feared the glowing eyes would return. She took her pistol from the top of the nightstand, just in case.

But the intruders didn't return that night. Nor the night after. Tina Brandt never saw the glowing eyes again.

The day after her terrifying experience, Tina told of her experience to a close friend.

"There was a storm last night," he told her, "lightning and thunder. I've heard of a phenomenon called ball lighting that sometimes occurs during thunderstorms. Spheres of light shoot through the air, and when they vanish they sometimes make a big exploding noise. That might have been what you saw last night."

"No," Tina said. "I've heard of that, too. Ball lightning doesn't come through a closed window. And it doesn't paralyze you while it moves slowly around the room!"

"Then what could it have been?"

"I wish I knew," Tina replied nervously. "I just hope that I never see it again!"

She hasn't seen the eyes since then. But the anticipation that she might forces her to sleep with the light on every night—just like fear compelled her to do when she was just a child.

DEVIL MAY CARE

Around the turn of the twentieth century new inventions were being introduced to consumers at an incredible pace. Country people, used to the old ways and not understanding that new machines would make their work easier, sometimes considered innovations like the automobile, the steam tractor, and the electric milker, as infernal. The ethic of hard work suggested that work-saving devices underlined the basic philosophy that idle hands were the devil's handmaiden.

Superstitious country folk made up stories about the new inventions, intimating, perhaps, that these were creations of the devil. The following is such a tale from Tennessee's flatlands—the story of a fiendish auto and the fate of one man who just had to find out what made it tick.

It was one of those hot, shimmering days in August when Miss Prunella rolled into Jackson in her brand new automobile. At first the townspeople saw nothing strange about the car. Autos were not totally new to Jackson, but there were few of them around. And it stood to reason that if anyone was going to buy one of the newfangled, horse scaring gadgets, it would be Miss Prunella.

But some thought it was strange that her car operated so quietly, not the usual chugging and backfiring associated with an auto. In fact it soon became likely to all that Miss

Prunella was running on empty—that no telltale signs of the internal combustion engine were associated with her strange new vehicle.

Miss Prunella was considered a bit strange, herself, by the townspeople. Indeed, some thought she was a witch. She filled the classic stereotype of a witch. She was a very old woman, with a long hooked nose—she even had a large wart perched on the end of it. She dressed in somber, dark clothing, and her voice possessed the resonance of something between a cack and a cackle.

She lived far out in the country, away from everyone, in an old house in desperate need of repair. Some said a hundred black cats roamed freely around the grounds and through the house, looking on while she mixed up mysterious potions and cast troublesome spells.

Therefore, no one really thought it very unusual to imagine that Miss Prunella was driving an automobile without benefit of gasoline. Some of the locals even came to the conclusion that the car ran by the power of pure evil—that Satan, himself, was pushing from the rear. But they were thankful, on the other hand, that loud noises were not frightening the horses.

When Miss Prunella pulled up to the board sidewalk, one brave soul remarked how much he admired her new car.

Miss Prunella smiled and said, "It's the latest. An electric." And then, as if reading his mind, she added, "It don't need no gas. It runs off a battery."

Well, that at least explained the lack of noise.

The old woman visited town about once a week to load up on supplies. She walked into the general store, where she was practically the only patron who didn't buy on credit. She didn't need it. Her father, who had died many years before, had left her with enough money to keep her in luxury for the rest of her life.

While Miss Prunella shopped, curious onlookers made a visual inspection of her new automobile. It was painted black, of course, to match her outfits. Inside, the upholstery was also black. The dashboard was filled with shiny instruments and looked quite impressive.

"Do you think you'll ever own one of these?" one man asked his farmer friend standing beside him.

"Nope," the second man replied. "I'll keep my horse. Hay costs less than gas-o-line."

The first man grinned and moved closer to the window so he could see inside the car better. Something was written in yellow letters across the front of the dashboard. He motioned to his friend. "Can you read what that says?" he asked. "I left my spectacles at home."

The second man squinted into the darkness. "It says, 'Devil May Care.'" He turned with a quizzical expression. "I wonder what that means?"

"I think it means something like 'throw caution to the wind.' Or maybe even 'do what you dang well please.'"

Both men thought that was a strange thing to write on the dashboard of one's new automobile. When Miss Prunella emerged from the store, and while they were helping her load her automobile with groceries and other supplies, the first man asked her about it.

"Oh, that," she laughed. "That's what I named my car. Devil May Care."

"I see," he replied as he opened the back door and leaned inside to place her packages on the seat. Suddenly a rush of cold air enveloped him. Outside, it was summer, hot and muggy. Inside the car, it felt like the depths of winter.

Miss Prunella suspiciously watched her volunteer helpers from the corner of her eye. When they were finished, she smiled again and thanked the two men for helping her. Then she climbed into the driver seat and silently drove her car out of town.

The two men watched as the car disappeared around a corner. Then the first man told his friend about the cold temperature inside the auto. "There's something not right about that there car," he said.

"Maybe it was your imagination," his friend said.

"Maybe it was," the first man answered as he stared off into space. "But I'm going to find out one way or the other.

I'm going out there tonight and give that horseless carriage a good going over myself."

The heat of the day hung around even after the sun had gone down. The two men had traveled down a rutted country road, ten miles on horseback, when they finally spotted Miss Prunella's house looming up out of the darkness. A single light shone at the living room window.

"She's up late tonight," the first man said.

"I've heard she never sleeps at all," his friend answered. "Witches don't sleep."

The first man said nothing. Instead he dismounted, and his friend did the same. After tying their horses to a convenient tree limb, they slowly and silently stole through the thick brush to an isolated corner of the house.

Giant trees overhung the sparse lawn. Stones littered the ground. The men made their way around the house, being careful not to trip over any of the rocks at their feet. When they came to the lighted window, the first man raised up on his tiptoes and carefully peeked inside.

"Is she in there?" the friend asked.

"Yeah. She's sitting in a big chair reading a book."

"Well, you can bet it's not the Bible," the friend commented sarcastically.

The pair continued to work their way around the building. Finally, in front, they spied Devil May Care sitting majestically in the driveway.

A cloud drifted in front of the moon, which made the scene even more gloomy and spooky than before. A faint green glow came from the interior of the auto and gleamed through the windows.

"What's that from?" the friend asked, nodding toward the light.

"That's what we're going to find out," the first man replied. The men picked up their feet and began running toward the automobile. When they were twenty feet away, they slowed down and approached more cautiously. The friend looked back over his shoulder to make sure no one was watching.

Then the pair stopped. The glow inside the vehicle was coming from all directions at once—not from any single source like a bulb or a flame. Furthermore, now that they were closer, they noticed the car was filled with a light mist—just like fog.

The friend put his hand on the first man's arm. "I don't think I like this very much," he said nervously. "I really do want to get out of here and come back tomorrow."

But the first man would not be swayed. He reached for the door handle and opened it a crack. Mist seeped out.

He opened the door a little more.

More mist.

Finally he gathered enough courage to open the door all the way. The interior continued to glow green as he bent down so he could get a clear view of the ceiling to find the source of the light. Nothing there.

"I'm going to get inside this thing," he told his friend.

The friend got a panicked look on his face. "I wouldn't do that if I were you."

"Nonsense," the first man said. "After all, it's only a car."

As he stooped down to slide onto the seat he noticed, once again, the legend "Devil May Care" scrawled on the dashboard. What an odd name for an automobile, he probably thought to himself as he sat on the seat.

The friend backed away a few steps.

Suddenly the door of the car slammed shut without benefit of human assistance. The first man's eyes widened in surprise. The light turned from green to red, then to deep purple. A whining sound was heard from inside as the man's hands shot to his throat. His friend watched in horror as the mist rapidly engulfed the man inside the car; and then, in a moment, he was gone.

The friend rushed forward and tried to open the door, but it would not budge. The whining sound suddenly died down and the light inside returned to its "normal" green color. Then the mist disappeared.

A voice behind the second man made him jump. He whirled around in time to see Miss Prunella standing at the doorway of her house.

"I see your friend was not very good at taking warnings," she said as she scowled at him. "It was as plain as the nose on your face."

"W-what warning?" the friend stammered as he started backing away.

"You see," she said, "that automobile was a gift from a friend of mine in payment for all the work I've done for him over the years—a sort of payment for services rendered. Your friend should not have been so nosy. I tried to warn him with the message."

"The message?"

"Of course. 'Devil may care.' Don't get too close if you know what's good for you."

The friend threw out his arms in disbelief. "But he's gone. Disappeared. Where did he go to."

Miss Prunella cackled. "Since he was so curious about my automobile, I sent him to the source, where he could get firsthand information. Now he knows all he wanted to know about it."

"But where?" the friend asked.

Miss Prunella cackled again. "Simple," she answered. "You might say that your curious friend got in way over his head, and now he's 'gone to the Devil.'"

THE GHOST WHO WANTED A HUG

Who remembers the forgotten grave
In a tangle of woodland?
Beneath the soil lie the bones
Of one of the forgotten, to lie in peace
Until the final calling.
But wait!
The spirit is restless
It hungers for companionship
And love.

Buried beneath Tennessee's sod are the bones of men and women who are remembered only by hasty notations in dusty family Bibles. Most tragic of all are children who died before they came into their full promise.

I remember one name that I came across while reading through a register in an old Bible. The list was full of names, dates, and places—births, marriages, and deaths—records that were pretty complete.

Then I saw a single notation scrawled in pencil in a margin. "Jenny M. d. 11½ years." That was it—an incomplete name, and age at death. When I questioned the owner of the Bible, he had no earthly idea who Jenny M. was. "She might not have been a member of my family," he said. "You'll notice the last initial is different than mine. Of course, that could have stood for a middle name."

"Have you ever tried to track Jenny M. down?" I asked.

"Yeah," he replied. "I once spent a couple of days looking around the local graveyards, but I didn't find anything. Who knows where she's buried, or even if there was such a person in the first place. No one in my family knows who she was."

Jenny M. has haunted me for years. Who was she? Did she have hair the color of sunshine, or as black as a raven's? Were her eyes blue or brown or something in between? What did she like the most? What did she like the least? Did someone dry her tears when she was sad, or hold her close when she was frightened? Was Jenny M. loved while she lived, and was she mourned when she died?

With the exception of the fact that she died in her twelfth year, all I know for sure about Jenny M. is her first name—and even that might be a nickname. Tragically, as far as history is concerned, Jenny M. might as well have never been born!

How many more Jenny M.'s are there in Tennessee?

Scattered throughout the state are thousands of lost graves—unkempt family plots grown thick with weeds and shrub—ignored over the years. Many more are isolated single graves, long forgotten by the living. Do the tiny bones of my Jenny M. lie in one of those lonely pits—maybe even in unconsecrated ground?

The following is a tale about one such lost grave and the ghost of the little girl who inhabited it.

A patch of woods near Hickory Valley, in the southwestern part of Tennessee, is said to be haunted by the ghost of a little girl who died over a century ago.

No one knows her name, and there is no official record of her existence. But a rude stone marker deep in the woods stands sentinel to the fact that someone lies buried there. The inscription, if indeed there was one carved there at all, has long ago fallen to the elements.

A local legend has grown up around that lonely grave. Nearby there is another tombstone—that of a woman killed during the War Between The States. Could this second grave be that of the mother? Here's the legend as one person told it to me.

An old man once lived in a nearby cabin on the main road into town. He had fought in the Civil War in his youth, unfortunately on the side of the Yankees—an unforgivable sin in that part of Tennessee. After the peace was signed, the war-weary veteran returned home to encounter the overwhelming displeasure of his Southern neighbors.

"How could you go off and fight for that long-legged ape Lincoln?" they asked.

"Didn't believe in secession," he tried to explain. "I fought for what I believed in."

Of course his explanation didn't quell the disgust one little bit. To make things worse for everyone, his young wife and child had been murdered when his marauding Yankee "buddies" had sacked the town. Afterward the bodies were secretly buried by townspeople sympathetic to the family, but not to the "traitor." So that he would not desecrate their graves by visiting them, he was never told where his family was buried.

Former friends shunned the veteran and even threatened violence. The fellow decided that it was no use to try to live in town. Instead he moved to a little patch of land he owned in the county, built a small cabin, and spent the rest of his long life in forced seclusion.

His years in exile passed slowly. But occasionally he was visited by a traveler who was ignorant of his host's past. At these times the old man served the stranger a simple supper, offered him his barn to sleep in, and then talked far into the night to try to find out the latest news from the outside world.

One night he heard a gentle rapping at his door. *Ah,* he thought to himself. *A visitor.* When he opened the door he found a little girl of about three years old standing on his porch, looking up at him with big, sorrowful eyes.

"Who are you?" the old man asked. "Are you lost?"

The child shook her head. Then without waiting for an

invitation, she walked into the cabin. She moved to the fire and sat down on a wooden stool beside it.

The little girl watched the old man as he moved to the fireplace. Over the flames hung an iron kettle filled with pungent rabbit stew. The old man sat down. He looked first at his little visitor, then at the stew pot. There was something familiar about her. Was she a neighbor's child who he had seen on one of his infrequent forays into town to buy supplies?

There was a faraway, lifeless look in her black eyes. She wore a rust-colored dress and no shoes. Her hair was a dirty blonde color.

"You hungry?" he asked.

The little girl nodded that she wasn't.

"Then, what is it that you want? Are you lost?"

She shook her head and continued watching him. It looked like she was shivering. The old man had an old brown shawl that he kept for cold nights. After rummaging through a pile of old clothes, he found the garment and carefully placed it around her shoulders. She smiled, stood up, walked over to him, put her small arms around his neck, and squeezed him as tightly as she could.

The old man felt an inner warmth that he had not felt in years. When the child returned to the stool he asked, "Where is your mother and father?"

The child didn't answer. Instead she stood up, smiled, and turned toward the door. Then without waiting for him to open it for her, she walked right through it!

Panic seized the old man. What had he seen? A ghost?

He ran to the door and threw it open. He searched the area around his cabin, looking for some trace of the little girl, but he found nothing. Then he slowly returned to his cabin, shut the door behind him, and threw the wooden bolt that locked it.

The next morning the old man thought he might walk to town. He hadn't set foot in the place for over six months and wondered about the kind of reception he would get.

It took him about two hours to travel the five miles to town. When he arrived, the first thing he noticed was how everything had changed. There were new buildings and new businesses. And the town was much larger now than he remembered. There must have been a sudden boom.

He had a little money in his pocket, so he decided to visit a general store to pick up a few supplies. When he walked through the double wooden doors into the dark interior, the first thing he saw was a half dozen men sitting in chairs, gathered around an old black stove. Since it was summer, of course there was not a fire.

All turned their attention to him as he walked through the door. Almost immediately a young man asked, "You're Hugh Street, ain't you?"

The old man nodded his head.

"Figured you were," the younger man replied. "You ain't been to town much, but I've heard plenty about you."

Sensing that trouble was brewing, the old man nervously turned to the counter and eyed a jar of peppermint sticks sitting beside a wooden box that was filed with nut-brown plugs of chewing tobacco. The younger man continued talking while his companions listened intently to the conversation.

"My daddy said you fought with the Yankees in the late rebellion. He said you were a turncoat."

The old man tried to ignore the younger man. The clerk approached, and the old man pointed to the jar of peppermint sticks.

"I'll have one of those," he said.

The clerk removed the jar lid and tilted the glass toward the old man, who took one of the candies. Then he reached into his pocket and pulled out a penny and gave it to the clerk.

"Is that true?" the young man persisted. "If you are the same Mr. Street, there is something I have to talk to you about."

The old man turned slowly toward the group of men and leaned defiantly against the counter. "Yes, I did," he growled. "I fought for the side I thought was right."

The younger man smiled. "I surely do admire a man who stands up for what he believes in," he said.

One of his companions turned to the young man and scowled. "Well I don't," he said emphatically. "Especially when a man fights against his own kin." Then he turned to the old man. "How many of our brothers did you kill in all them battles, Street?"

The old man glared at his detractor. "Don't know," he shot back defiantly. "Never counted."

An uneasy silence settled over the interior of the old store. After a moment the young man stood up and walked over to the counter.

"Don't you fret over them, Mr. Street," he said. "This is 1901. The war's been over almost forty years."

The old man said nothing in return. Instead he continued to glare at the men seated around the stove. The young fellow carefully picked a peppermint out of the glass jar and handed a penny to the clerk. Then he began to chew on the end of the sweet-tasting candy stick.

"Don't reckon you aim to stay in here much longer," the young man said. "Leastwise I don't see much of a point in it, considering all the hard feelings."

There was something about this young man that the old man trusted, but he couldn't quite put his finger on it. The young man smiled and said, "I would like to chat with you for a while if you don't mind, Mr. Street."

The old man nodded his head. It had been so long since he had someone to talk to that he decided he would take a chance and accompany the young fellow.

Both men walked out of the store and into the street. The young man pointed to a ragged buckboard and a mangy old horse that was tied up next to the boardwalk. He smiled again. "It don't look like much," he said, "but she's all I got. Leastwise, it's better than walking."

The two men climbed into the wagon. The young man snapped the reins, and the horse turned to look at the driver, a sorrowful look in its cloudy white eyes.

"Go on," the young man urged gently. "It's not very far."

The horse turned like it understood exactly what the driver was saying, and slowly walked down the main street and out of the town.

It was a beautiful summer day, not too hot or muggy. The sun shone brightly from an azure-blue sky. Birds flew overhead. The mangy horse plodded steadily down the rutted, dusty road like it knew exactly where it was going. Apparently there was no need to give the horse any direction.

A short distance from town the young man said, "I hope you have a little time to see what I got to show you, Mr. Street."

The old man nodded uneasily. "What is it?" he asked.

The young man pointed to a patch of woods to their right. "Over there," he said. "In those woods."

The horse veered off the road. The wagon crossed a little meadow and was soon deep in the cool woods. Presently the wagon halted and the young man jumped off. He stood waiting for the old man, who was hesitant about getting off. He was starting to get nervous about the whole mystery.

"It's all right, sir," the younger man reassured him. "We're not going far now."

The old man climbed down from the wagon. Then he looked around. The young man pointed to a tangle of underbrush about thirty yards in front of them. "What I want to show you is in there," he said.

"You don't know me, but my father knew you well before the Civil War. In fact it was he who gave his daughter in marriage to you. I am Albert, his last son, born after you returned home, and my father had buried my sister."

The old man suddenly looked like all the wind had been taken out of his sails. He stared at his brother-in-law that he had never seen.

"I left home to attend college in Nashville and I've only come back in the past week. My home is there.

"I never visited you because my father forbade it. Furthermore, he made me promise never to tell you the location of the graves." Then the young man smiled and pointed. "But in those weeds are buried the bodies of your wife and child. Since I hold no grudges, I thought I'd show you where they were."

Tears welled up in the old man's eyes. After all these years of wondering, the graves had been right under his nose all the time—right on the main road between his house and the town.

"How can I ever thank you?" he said to the young man.

The young man said nothing. Instead he turned to walk back to the wagon. Then he climbed into the seat to wait. The old man turned again toward the tangle of brush and began walking slowly toward it.

When he stood ten feet away he saw the top of one of the stones peeking out though the tall weeds, but saw no other. *Maybe someone made off with the second stone*, he thought.

He bent down and parted the weeds from the front of the stone. There, roughly carved, was the name of his wife and her dates.

He turned and began looking for the grave of his child, but he could see nothing. Then a glint of white, lying close to the ground, caught his eye. He moved ten feet to his right and suddenly froze in his tracks. His heart leapt into his throat.

It was a tombstone all right—his daughter's. And he suddenly realized the reason why it had not been as visible as his wife's. Draped over the top of the stone was his old brown shawl.

There have been a number of variations of this story. Another tale tells of a little girl hitchhiking on the road in the middle of a violent rainstorm. When a kindly motorist stops to give her a lift, he offers the shivering girl his coat for warmth. Then the little girl directs him to her house, but when he arrives she has disappeared. He goes to the house, raps, and an old couple open the door. When the motorist tells them about his passenger, the old woman tells him of her little "Mary" who died years ago. Of course the motorist doesn't believe her. The old woman offers proof by taking him to her daughter's grave. To the motorist's horror, he finds his coat draped over the tombstone.

The same basic story was also immortalized years ago by the bluegrass group, The Country Gentleman, in their recording of "Bringing Mary Home."

A FATE WORSE THAN DEATH

I believe there are as many "Lovers' Lane" tales as there are sands on the beach. Certainly these stories have been around for years—ever since the first boy took the first girl to a secluded spot in the woods for a little serious flirtation.

Lovers' Lane tales all have one thing in common. They were created for the express purpose of scaring the female so badly that she had no other choice than to hunker up next to her male companion for protection. And as we all know, there is nothing as cavalier as a young man whose girlfriend is scared out of her gourd!

I remember my grandfather telling me of a young lady that he was courting, just before the beginning of the twentieth century. He had just built his first surrey—Papaw was a wagon maker, among other things—and he decided to take the vehicle down the road for its maiden run. There was a girl that he was interested in, so he stopped by her house to see if she was game for a ride in the moonlight.

It was late in the evening, and the girl's parents were understandably suspicious of my grandfather's intentions. But they knew his parents, and Papaw's reputation in the neighborhood was fairly honorable. So they allowed her to accompany him.

This was the first time the couple had been together alone, so the pair sat far apart on the seat.

At first, my grandfather impressed his companion with a

glowing account of how he came to build his proud new sur-
rey. She seemed duly overwhelmed by his creation, yet
remained on her side of the seat. So Papaw did what genera-
tions of males before and after him did when they wanted to
entice a young lady to sit close.

He told her a scary story.

Many years later Papaw confessed to me that he could not
remember the exact yarn but confirmed that it involved a homi-
cidal maniac roaming the country, looking for teenagers to
carve up with his long knife. The ruse was successful. The
young lady, whose name was Edna, scooted across the seat
and nestled close to Papaw for protection.

And that was the way they drove home—Papaw with my
future grandmother's head resting comfortably on his shoul-
der! Where would I be today if it had not been for that scary
tale Papaw told so long ago on a moonlit night?

Here is a "Lovers' Lane" tale from West Tennessee. I won-
der how many lovers this one has brought together?

Eternal rest is not in the cards for Ol' Truly. Like the infamous Jacob Marley in the classic Charles Dickens story, *A
Christmas Carol,* Ol' Truly's tortured spirit was condemned to
walk the earth forever. But it is not the "chains he forged in
life" that tormented Truly's rotted-out hulk. Rather it was a
curse placed on him by his dying girlfriend.

In happier times John Truly was star quarterback of his
high school football team. Twice Tennessee state champi-
ons, the team was the pride of the quiet farm town near the
Mississippi River where Truly lived with his widowed mother.

Like so many other small towns across America, the local
high school football team was the cornerstone of civic pride.
Football season heralded the welding of the town's citizens
into a common bond. Even political differences were forgotten as the hometown team swept onto the field. All anyone
really cared about was a winning team.

When the team lost, the next day's mood in town was as
black as the infernal pit. But when the team won (as it usu-

ally did) there was great rejoicing and dancing in the streets.

Much of the team's success was due to young Truly's prowess with a football. His forward passes flew straight into the waiting grasp of the receiver who, invariably, was poised within an easy sprint to the goal posts. Truly's completion rate approached sixty percent—amazing when one considers the large number of passes he threw in a season.

By the time Truly turned high school junior, his delighted coach had already predicted that he would turn pro. Letters poured in from colleges and universities offering Truly full athletic scholarships to play football. And his name and picture always appeared in the Memphis newspaper.

As Truly's fame grew, so did his ego. Truly's vanity centered around his physique—an Adonis-like body that rippled with bulging muscles. He stood over six feet tall, with fair hair and heavy-lidded blue eyes that made girls giddy with delight.

He could have had the pick of any girl in school. But Truly's attention was focused on one young lady in particular who, like himself, was an exceptional beauty.

She was tall and lithe. Her hair was the color of ripe blackberries. Her figure was a marvel of structural engineering. She was a varsity cheerleader. Her name was Elizabeth, but everyone called her Beth. Some folks even called her "Evil Beth" or "Devil Beth."

Beth was both desirable and frightening. Her preoccupation with the occult bordered on obsession. When not clothed in bright cheerleader's garb, she donned somber clothes—either black or dark shades of gray. She looked very much the role she apparently was trying to play—that of a witch.

Beth claimed to practice both black and white magic and firmly believed she was a reincarnation of the Widow Goodspeed, an accused witch who was hanged, then burned, in seventeenth century England. Some folks in town believed her. They had good reason.

Terrible things sometimes happened to people who crossed her. A neighbor who complained to the police of strange noises and lights coming from the old barn behind her house once fell sick with a mysterious ailment that no doctor could diagnose. Children who mocked her took unexplained falls from their bicycles or fell out of trees that they were trying to climb.

Other things happened. Sometimes when Beth spoke angrily, her normally musical voice would appear to be replaced with another—the raspy voice of an old woman speaking in an antiquated Elizabethan English accent. Times like this would send shivers up the spine of the listener.

Most of the boys her age stayed out of Beth's way. But there was something about her mysterious behavior that fascinated Truly. He felt himself strangely attracted to her.

At first Beth ignored the handsome Truly. But Truly was persistent, and mutual feelings slowly developed between the two. Eventually Truly and Beth became an item on the high school campus.

Months passed. Spring turned to summer. Truly usually worked at a local feed and grain store during summer recess to help out at home, but this year he didn't. He had more pressing interests.

Mrs. Truly was worried. Her son was spending entirely too much time with his mysterious girlfriend. But there was little she could do about it. Whenever she brought up the subject, Truly would fly into an uncontrollable rage—quite out of character for the amiable young man. Truly's mother thought Beth was holding a powerful influence over her son.

Furthermore, rumors bounced around town that Truly and Beth had formed an unholy alliance and were practicing black magic in the ramshackle barn behind Beth's house. Strange colored lights had been seen coming from the barn.

When the next football season rolled around, Truly failed to appear for practice. His frustrated coach tried to reason with him. But Truly explained he wasn't interested in football anymore, especially since Beth no longer was a member of the cheerleading squad. (She had been dropped for failing to show up for practice.)

As the school year started, it seemed that Truly was committed to little else but Beth. His grades slipped, and he was in serious danger of flunking the first semester of his senior year.

One night in November, just before Thanksgiving, the townspeople were treated to an unusual but dazzling display of the northern lights. The sky was brilliant with a rainbow of colors—blues, reds, and greens. They shimmered and changed shapes. Nothing like it had ever been seen in Tennessee. Northern lights were usually reserved only for Arctic skies.

The next day Truly announced to anyone who would listen to him that he and Beth had conjured up the lights by working magic. He told the townspeople that another performance of the lights would appear two days hence to prove his claim. Sure enough, on Sunday night the lights appeared again—this time even more brilliant and colorful than before.

"A fluke," the townspeople said.

"Coincidence."

"Dumb luck."

How could a mere mortal create such a dazzling display in the heavens. That was the province of God!

"You don't believe me, do you, Mom?" Truly said to his mother.

"Of course I don't!" his mother replied sharply. "When are you going to get this magic foolishness out of your head and go back to your studies?"

But Truly would not be put off so easily. "Look up in the sky at eleven tomorrow night, Mom. You will see the lights again, and this time you, and the whole town, will believe."

An hour before midnight the following day, the town saw the lights overhead for the third time. The town believed all right, but their reaction to the lights unexpectedly raged out of control.

One of the local preachers, a hellfire and brimstone firebrand, was absolutely convinced the good town citizens of his community were dealing with not just one witch, but a pair of them. At the next Wednesday night prayer meeting, he preached his sermon based on the Biblical verse which said, "Thou shalt not suffer a witch to live." He made it quite apparent that he was ready to go out on his own witch-hunt and flush the varmints out of town—that is, if he could find a dozen men with the guts to go with him.

The preacher continued to preach against the pair, repeatedly accusing them of witchcraft. The parents of both children consulted lawyers but found most attorneys in town were loath to buck the powerful preacher and his congregation.

As the hellfire and brimstone sermons continued, Beth was overheard by some of her schoolmates to defiantly say that the preacher would get his one day. The controversy did not seem to be affecting her activities one little bit.

But Truly was growing nervous at the town's attitude toward his and Beth's hocus pocus. He thought seriously about giving up the relationship and trying to reenter the mainstream of town life.

That night he was to meet with Beth in the old barn behind her house. There he would tell her that it was all over between them. Of course no one knows exactly what was said or the girl's reaction, but the next day Beth vanished without a trace.

A few nights later the preacher and a few hardcore members of his congregation met Truly walking down the street. To his horror, Truly discovered the men were armed with pistols. They had been looking for Beth. Apparently the preacher had found men willing to go on his witch-hunt.

The preacher bolted from the car and grabbed Truly by the arm. "All right, boy," he growled. "Where is she?"

"Who?" Truly asked innocently.

"That blaspheming woman you've been hanging around with."

Truly's eyes darted around the street, looking for a cop to rescue him. But it was late and the street was nearly deserted. He turned to the preacher. "I-I don't know," Truly stammered.

"You're lyin'."

The preacher drew his pistol and pressed the cold muzzle against Truly's head. Another man held the boy's arms behind him.

"Now tell me where she is or I'll blow your head off," the preacher growled. His breath was foul with whiskey. Apparently prayer was not the only thing that fortified him and gave him courage. "Only a witch would protect another witch," he continued.

Beads of sweat rolled off Truly's face even though it was a chilly November night. "I am not a witch," he protested loudly.

"Someone sure is. Someone burned down the church house earlier this evening, and I suspect it was you and your girlfriend that did it."

The muzzle of the pistol pressed even harder against Truly's temple.

"I don't know nothing about a fire," Truly protested.

"Save your own soul before it's too late," the preacher slurred in a voice loud enough to reach the heavens. "Tell me where she is. I can help you. We'll pray together. You don't have to suffer eternal damnation because of her."

One of the men in the group murmured a fervent "Amen."

"B-but," Truly stammered again, "I took a solemn oath...."

"An oath not to tell where she was?" The preacher raised his eyebrows. "A devil's oath, I'll wager. Blasphemy from one minion of Hell to the other."

"I really don't know where she is," Truly pleaded. "All she said to me was that she was leaving town for a few days. Now please, let me go."

But the preacher cocked the hammer of his pistol and pressed the muzzle even harder against Truly's head. "Tell me where she is!" he demanded. "You have ten seconds before I blow your head all over this street."

Suddenly the men heard a voice from the shadows. It sounded like a woman's voice, but was deep and rasping.

"You be looking for me, Reverend?" the voice asked.

The preacher wheeled in the direction of the voice and saw Beth's tall and lanky figure emerge from the shadows. For an uncomfortable moment everyone stood and stared at her. Then Beth's eyes began to glow. She raised her arm and pointed a bony finger toward the preacher.

"Art thou he who doth fight the forces of evil with his tongue? Or art thou a man of courage who fights Satan with an eye for an eye?"

"What kind of talk is that, Preacher?" one of the men turned and asked.

"The talk of the Devil, Brother," the preacher replied.

"And art thou he who doth challenge the forces of evil with that pathetic weapon in thy hand?" Beth continued. "Shall I call upon the furies to descend on thee?"

The preacher turned to Truly. "What's she saying?"

Truly shook his head. "I don't know. I've never heard that kind of talk from her before!"

"ALL WILL DIE!" Beth screamed as her face contorted beyond all recognition.

The men gasped at the sight and began to retreat—all except the preacher. "Come back here, you cowards!" he demanded. But it was too late. Only the preacher, Truly, and Beth were left standing on the street.

"Art thou going to shoot him, Reverend?" Beth asked in a rasping voice and nodding toward the gun pointed at Truly's head.

The preacher was shaking with fear by now. His courage had drained from his body. He had preached against evil all his life, but to be confronted with the personification of it was something he hadn't reckoned on.

"Get back," he said in a quavering voice, "or I will shoot."

Then Beth laughed an evil laugh. "Do ye think I care what happens to him?" she said. "Or to thee?"

"Beth, get out of here!" Truly shouted. "He's going to kill you!"

Beth turned to Truly and laughed. "It looks like ye be in more danger than I," she said scornfully. "If ye weren't so spineless ye would help me. Use the skills I taught thee. KILL HIM!"

Truly replied, "I won't. I won't kill anyone."

The preacher, his eyes crazy with fear, looked at Truly. "What do you mean, kill me?"

"He could," Beth replied. "One word and ye would be consumed in the flames of Hell. But since he won't do it, I will...."

The preacher turned in a panic and fired at Beth. The bullet made a hollow thumping sound as it penetrated her skull—like a shot punching through a ripe melon. The girl screamed and fell to the street. Truly turned and ran toward her. The preacher froze in terror and dropped his gun to the pavement.

With such a wound, Beth should have been killed instantly. But she was still alive. Truly cradled her head in his lap. She looked up at him. Hate burned in her eyes.

"Why didn't ye kill him?" she demanded to know.

"I couldn't," Truly answered. "Now be quiet. We'll get you an ambulance...."

Beth laughed scornfully. "Ye poor fool. This body be already dead. It was dead on the day I entered it."

Truly thought that Beth was out of her head with pain. "Just be quiet. We'll get help."

Once again Beth laughed. "Fool! Do ye still not know who I be. I be the spirit of the Widow Goodspeed. When I find a young one who is a willing vessel..."

"...you possess it," the preacher finished.

Beth glanced at the preacher and chuckled evilly. "Ye cannot destroy evil. That is only for the Ancient of Days. I will simply leave this body and pass on to another. This one is no good to me now. But first I must repay ye, Reverend, for the inconvenience thou hast caused me."

Suddenly the preacher's eyes went back in his head so only the whites showed. His body began shaking violently. He opened his mouth to scream, but nothing came out. He sank to the pavement, his muscles quivering. Then he was still.

Truly watched in horrified fascination. "My God!" he muttered. Then he turned to Beth. She grinned at him.

"God hath nothing to do with it," she cackled. "God despises the hypocrite and the Devil hates a coward. And my 'father' has saved you a just reward. You will die and, then, you will live—that is the greatest curse anyone could put upon you. Your body will rot as in the grave, but no grave shall ever hold you. You are condemned to walk the earth forever."

Then Truly felt Beth's body go limp. And from thin air he heard the cackling laughter of the Widow Goodspeed, slowly growing fainter in the distance.

From the darkness, Truly then heard an ambulance siren in the night air. The police arrived soon after. The bodies of the preacher and the girl were gathered up and taken to the morgue. Truly was arrested for both murders, tried as an adult, convicted, and sentenced to life imprisonment.

But prison life didn't agree with him, and one day a horrified jailer found him hanging in his cell. His body was buried in the small graveyard where his family had attended church for years.

The next Sunday, after the funeral, his mother arrived at church early to put flowers on her son's grave. To her horror she discovered that someone had dug up her son's body. The authorities were notified and a search was initiated, but the body was never recovered.

Upon inspecting the opened grave, the sheriff noted that rather than being dug up, the pit looked as if someone had pushed the dirt out from within.

Where was Truly's body. No one knew. But there were theories. One of the most popular was that someone had objected to a suspected witch, and convicted murderer, being buried in consecrated ground. They had stolen into the cemetery and removed the body.

But there were other reports coming in from the neighborhood—sightings of a horribly rotting man roaming the woods at night. He especially frequented favorite spots where lovers would park their cars and enjoy each other's company.

One couple was parked in the woods, a few yards from the bank of the Mississippi River. It was a dark night—only the sliver of a full moon was hanging in the sky.

The lovemaking was getting a bit too passionate, and the girl pulled away to catch her breath. When she glanced out the window she saw a horrible, decayed face peering at her through the window. She screamed.

The creature began pounding the closed window. The boy tried to start the car, but the motor would not fire. The girl screamed again. The motor roared to life, and the driver jammed it into gear and sped away.

All the way back home, the boy broke the speed limit. Finally he pulled into his girlfriend's driveway. Although still terribly frightened, she had calmed down considerably. He put his arm around her shoulders.

"It's okay," he said soothingly. "You're home now."

"Its face was horrible," she sobbed. "It was like a corpse."

"Nonsense," the boy said. "What you saw was one of the bums that live near the river. They're all up and down the banks. It's a good thing we wasn't robbed."

The girl turned indignant. "No, it wasn't one of them!" she shouted. "It was a corpse that attacked the car!"

The boy smiled benevolently. "A good night's sleep will put this all behind you," he said. "By morning you'll forget that it ever happened."

Then he opened the door and hopped out of the car. He walked around to the passenger side to let his girlfriend out. But when he reached for the door he froze in horror when he saw a rotted hand still clinging to the handle!

As many readers will notice, this story is another variation of the most famous Lovers' Lane tale of all—"The Hook." Again two lovers in the woods come upon a homicidal maniac who tries to get into the car. The man, according to the story, slashed people to death with a steel hook that had replaced his severed hand. The lovers escape the killer, but when they return home they find that the man's hook still clings to the door handle. I don't know about anyone else, but I like the former story much better. It sounds to me like a tale that might have been printed in one of those creepy horror comic books of the 1950s.

The Deification of St. Elvis of Presley, or... LONG "LIVE" THE KING!

The "King of Rock and Roll" is dead, according to the official records of Shelby County. But to his legion of devoted fans, Elvis Presley is very much alive and is liable to pop up anywhere in the world.

Like in a Memphis hot doggery...

Like on the Riviera...

Like on the streets of Nashville...

Like on the beach at Waikiki...

...and in a thousand other far-flung locations.

Sightings of the King provide endless fodder for supermarket tabloids. Hardly a month goes by without at least one scandal sheet reporting that Elvis is still among the living. For instance, a Florida-based tabloid newspaper once informed its astonished readers that Elvis was alive and well, and rooming with John F. Kennedy!

Elvis's cult status is equal to, or exceeds, that of other legendary performers—Marilyn Monroe, James Dean, Thelma Todd, and Rudolph Valentino—who have managed to garner more notoriety dead than alive. The principle is simple. When the personality is larger than life, the legend seems to take on a life of its own.

The question is, however, *Is Presley still alive or really a ghost?* Strangely, no one has seriously tried to find out. Whatever the origins of these mysterious sightings, the visions are treated in the same way as visions of God or the

Virgin Mary—with cautious reverence.

Born in Tupelo, Mississippi, in 1935, Presley cannot be considered a native-born Tennessean. But Mississippi and Arkansas in the early 1950s were spawning grounds for pioneer rock singers like Presley, Carl Perkins, and Jerry Lee Lewis.

These were performers who blended rock and roll with country music, creating a whole new sound called rockabilly. They immigrated to West Tennessee because of an obscure little recording studio located at 706 Union Avenue in Memphis.

In Sam Phillips's Memphis Recording Service, Presley cut ten sides which were released by Sun Records. It was fortunate that Presley contacted Phillips at the beginning of his career. Major labels like RCA or Columbia probably would not have taken the time to develop that unknown something Elvis's singing style possessed—a bluesy cross between a black urban hipster and a country singer.

Elvis got his share of notoriety in the early days of his career. He was denounced from some church pulpits as being a degenerate, a gyrating corrupter of youth. Elvis's suggestive body gyrations gave social reformers a potent argument against the rising popularity of rock and roll in general. In 1956, when Elvis appeared on "The Ed Sullivan Show," camera operators were instructed to photograph the singer from the waist up to mask his quaking anatomy from an innocent television audience of swooning teenage girls. (Actually Elvis claimed his infamous hip action was the result of his natural reaction to music and that he was totally unaware of it while singing.)

The success of Elvis was definitely unsettling to the more puritanical elements in America. The fact that he was suddenly drafted into the Army in 1958, at the height of his fame, was construed by some supporters as a conservative-centered effort to take the King out of circulation for a while. Let him cool his heels in the Army for two years and his fans will forget him.

Not!

Upon his discharge from the Army, Elvis found himself more popular than ever. A career in the movies awaited—and more records.

When Elvis's brand of performance went out of style during the "British invasion" of the middle sixties and his teenaged fans tired of him, he performed in Las Vegas and entertained their mothers. He performed in Vegas for years, stopped making movies, and eventually seemed to lose his taste for his rock and roll music roots, except to occasionally perform one of his golden oldies. In fact, he mostly sang songs more suited to Tom Jones and Engelbert Humperdinck than to the King of Rock and Roll.

Presley's sudden death in 1977 of an alleged drug overdose sent shockwaves through his legions of fans. The fact that he had plumped up like the Goodyear blimp, and was only a shadow of his former rock and roll self, made little difference to them. The King was dead, and a state of profound mourning was in order.

Never in America was there such wailing and gnashing of teeth. Elvis's funeral was overrun with mourning, hysterical fans. One woman even kept vigil outside the gates of Graceland because she was convinced the King would rise on the third day. She was determined to witness the miracle.

In the wake of his untimely death, Elvis's career took a posthumous shot in the arm. Suddenly everything "Elvis" took on value—old records, the earrings, bubble gum cards, the Victrolas, guitars—you name it. Dealers of collectibles searched attics and garages for half-forgotten Elvis memorabilia—plastic bound diaries, wallets, photo buttons, pocket calendars, and records. Movie theaters were scrounged for advertising one-sheets and lobby cards from Elvis's movies. Then dealers charged big bucks in the resale of the merchandise to eager collectors. Even Graceland, his home in Memphis, became a shrine, visited by thousands of pilgrims each year.

And, needless to say, the sightings of Elvis began with a vengeance.

Nearly two decades after his death, a large number of Elvis

fans continues to be in a state of denial. "Elvis is still among us," they argue. "I don't care what the death certificate says!"

Is Elvis really alive and well and living with John F. Kennedy? Or did he remove himself to a remote island in the Mediterranean to flee persistent fans? Is he alive or dead? Questions answered eighteen years ago are still being asked by those who refuse to take "dead" for an answer.

But if the King is still alive, why would he fake his death and totally drop out of sight?

"It's all quite logical," a psychologist friend of mine told me. (He discussed his tongue-in-cheek theory only on the promise that I wouldn't reveal his name, embarrass him, and cause him the chastisement of his profession.) "Elvis didn't want his public to see him grow old. Can you imagine a sixty-year-old Elvis Presley throwing his back out of whack every time he swiveled?" An interesting theory and maybe not as far-fetched as it seems to be on the surface.

And speaking of theories, what about the suggestion that Elvis was murdered?

Conspiracy theories dog celebrities who suffer early deaths. Marilyn Monroe, for example was thought to be a victim of the Mafia. James Dean's car wreck was supposed to have been engineered by a jealous rival. Thelma Todd was said to have been murdered by the mob.

And who can count the conspiracy theories behind the assassination of President John F. Kennedy? Was it really Fidel Castro? The CIA? Or the FBI?

But who would want to assassinate the King of Rock and Roll?

The problem with the "live" sightings is that Elvis is supposed to look exactly as he did twenty years before his death. When the U.S. Postal Service issued an Elvis stamp recently, they ran a nationwide poll to determine if the public preferred a painting of the singer before or after Las Vegas. Overwhelmingly, the vote returned for the version featuring a young Elvis. Adoring fans are the victims of wishful thinking on the subject of Elvis. They prefer him trapped in time—forever young. Gods don't age, do they?

The sightings of a perpetually young Elvis, as some people theorized, may actually be that of his ghost. And why not a ghost of Elvis as he was, his mind unmuddled by drugs and his perfect body quivering with every downbeat.

One woman claimed Elvis, or a ghost that looked very much like him, once walked right through her on a Memphis street.

Another devoted fan claims that Elvis appeared to her one night at the foot of her bed. At the time, she was having marital problems and was undecided whether to leave her husband. Supposedly, Elvis sat down at her feet and talked the "situation" over with her. The pair spoke for ten minutes, and when the fan asked him to sing a chorus of "Hound Dog," the King suddenly disappeared.

On another occasion, Elvis was claimed to have been seen strolling down a Nashville street in broad daylight, clad in a white jumpsuit. Dozens of people saw him; and one fan, overcome by his presence, rushed up and asked for his autograph. This he cheerfully gave, then he vanished into the crowd.

When it suddenly dawned on the autograph hunter that her hero had been dead for years, she broke out in chill bumps. Did she actually see Elvis's ghost? Or was the man an impostor—one of a host of Elvis imitators who just happened to be gathered in Nashville that week for a convention?

Who knows? But as long as Elvis Presley lives in the hearts of his fans, he will continue to be found roaming the furthermost recesses of their most vivid memories.

Either way, the King of Rock and Roll lives!

Long "live" the King!

DARKMAN

I'll end our brief excursion into Tennessee ghostlore with one of the most unnerving "Black Aggie" stories that I've ever heard.

A Black Aggie is the apparition of a very evil person—usually a witch—who frequents graveyards in the dead of night. Nearly every town cemetery has at least one Aggie. The Aggie is instantly recognizable as a black ghost that looks like a floating shroud. It doesn't make a sound, and no features are usually discernible except the eyes.

A Black Aggie can be either a man or a woman, and it is usually up to no good. Seldom is one found whose mission in life is not to scare the daylights out of curious children. But there are exceptions as we will soon see.

The following tale is from Dyersburg.

The ghost called "Darkman" has been around for as long as anyone can remember. Even very old people remember hearing about Darkman from their parents. Some have even claimed to have seen him.

So we can safely assume Darkman has haunted this particular graveyard since before the turn of the twentieth century.

Those who have seen it in action all tell the same basic story. Darkman drifts out of the trees on moonlit nights and moves in silence to a certain tombstone on the south side of the cemetery. There he pauses, his hand poised over the grave. Then, without a sound, he turns and drifts back from whence he came. Darkman seems unaware of any observer who may be watching.

In life, Darkman was said to have been an evil miser who starved his wife and children while he stashed all of his money in a secret hiding place.

His family lived in a two-room shack, his children ran around in tatters, and his wife found herself fishing around the garbage to find enough for her family to eat. One time, according to the story, the youngest child had to be fed by a neighbor or it would have starved to death.

When the children were old enough, they left home. Soon afterward the miser's wife died—some say of neglect. The old man then became a total recluse, seldom venturing out into public. Neighbors said that he spent the rest of his days sitting in his shack and counting his money—over and over again.

When he died, no one—not even his children—attended the funeral. In fact, the authorities were hard-pressed to find even a clergyman willing to officiate. Finally, the sheriff, himself, had to say words over the grave, which was dug in the furthermost corner of the cemetery.

After the miser's death a concerted effort was made to find his stash of money. The rude shack he lived in was literally torn apart, and the ground surrounding it was dug up—but nothing was ever found, not even a cent.

As the years passed, Darkman's shade was seen more and more, silently gliding over the cemetery. It became quite a sport for town youngsters to hide behind a stone wall that surrounded part of the graveyard and watch for Darkman. They were almost never disappointed.

But something about Darkman's activities puzzled them, however. Why did he always do the same thing every night, and who was buried in the grave that he always visited?

One young fellow inspected the tombstone and found the writing on it almost obliterated. When he asked around town, no one had any idea who was buried there. It had been so long ago.

The fellow became so obsessed with Darkman and his activities that he determined to wait in the graveyard one night and see him for himself.

About ten o'clock a full moon rose over the trees and, sure enough, a black apparition emerged from the woods and began drifting over the cemetery. The young fellow held his breath. He had never seen Darkman before, and the first sight of him raised chill bumps all over his body.

The figure slowly sailed over the well-kept graves, stopping at one of the tombstones. The hand of the apparition raised. It seemed to be grasping something.

The young fellow thought that he saw something drop to the top of the monument.

Darkman slowly turned, floated back into the woods, and disappeared among the trees.

The fellow walked cautiously to the grave, all the while glancing uneasily toward the woods, lest the apparition return suddenly and surprise him.

When he reached the tombstone, he saw something glowing white, lying on top of the stone, which he recognized immediately. It was a large loaf of bread.

Then, as he watched, the loaf of bread slowly disappeared—just like it was sinking into the granite. In a short while it was gone.

The reality of what the young fellow had seen suddenly dawned on him. Darkman was a condemned soul. He had been so greedy and miserly in life that he was condemned to spend eternity doing good.

But who was he feeding with the bread? Certainly not the bones lying under the tombstone. Or was he?

Then the fellow realized the horrifying truth of what he had just seen. He was standing on the grave of Darkman's neglected wife!